Computational Terminology in NLP and Translation Studies (ConTeNTS 2023)

Varna, Bulgaria
7 September 2023

Editors:

Amal Haddad Haddad
Ayla Rigouts Terryn
Ruslan Mitkov

ISBN: 978-1-7138-9042-3

Printed from e-media with permission by:

Curran Associates, Inc.
57 Morehouse Lane
Red Hook, NY 12571

Some format issues inherent in the e-media version may also appear in this print version.

Association for Computational Linguistics
209 N. Eighth Street
Stroudsburg, Pennsylvania 18360

Phone: 1-570-476-8006
Fax: 1-570-476-0860

acl@aclweb.org

Additional copies of this publication are available from:

Curran Associates, Inc.
57 Morehouse Lane
Red Hook, NY 12571 USA
Phone: 845-758-0400
Fax: 845-758-2633
Email: curran@proceedings.com
Web: www.proceedings.com

Computational Terminology in NLP and Translation Studies (ConTeNTS)

Incorporating the 16th Workshop on Building and Using Comparable Corpora (BUCC)

associated with

The 14th International Conference on
Recent Advances in Natural Language Processing'2023

PROCEEDINGS

Edited by:
Amal Haddad Haddad, Ayla Rigouts Terryn and Ruslan Mitkov

Varna, Bulgaria
7 September, 2023
https://contents2023.kulak.kuleuven.be/
https://comparable.limsi.fr/bucc2023/

Computational Terminology in NLP and Translation Studies (ConTeNTS)
Incorporating the 16th Workshop on Building and Using Comparable Corpora (BUCC)
Associated with the International Conference
Recent Advances in Natural Language Processing'2023

PROCEEDINGS

7 September, 2023
https://contents2023.kulak.kuleuven.be/
https://comparable.limsi.fr/bucc2023/

e-book site: www.acl-bg.org

INCOMA Ltd.
Shoumen, BULGARIA

Preface

The 1st workshop on Computational Terminology in NLP and Translation Studies (ConTeNTs) was held in Varna, Bulgaria on the 7th of September 2023. This workshop was one of the events co-located with the RANLP 2023 conference (Recent Advances in Natural Language Processing) and incorporated the 16th Workshop on Building and Using Comparable Corpora (BUCC).

Computational Terminology, i.e., research on the automatic collection, management, and analysis of terminology, has attracted the interest of scholars with a diverse range of multidisciplinary backgrounds and motivations. This encompasses a broad spectrum of domains in Natural Language Processing (NLP) such as information retrieval, terminology extraction, question-answering systems, ontology building, machine translation, computer-aided translation, automatic or semi-automatic abstracting, text generation, etc. The field greatly benefits from insights from these different perspectives.

As terms contain a lot of specialised and domain-specific information, they are essential for knowledge mining from texts. Quick evolutions and new developments in specialised domains require efficient and systematic automatic term management. New terms need to be coined and translated to ensure the equitable development of domains in all languages. During the last decade, deep learning and neural methods have become the state of the art for most NLP applications. Those applications were shown to outperform previous methods on various tasks, including automatic term extraction, language mining, assessment of quality in machine translation, accessibility of terminology, etc.

Cross-lingual terminology research is an especially interesting field for both translators and interpreters, who often spend a lot of time and effort on terminology and can benefit from improved tools, and for computational linguists, for whom this is a challenging and interesting field that can offer insights into the latest (neural) techniques. Therefore, it made sense to incorporate the BUCC workshop, which focuses on the use of multilingual comparable corpora (more readily available than parallel corpora), and which hosted a shared task specifically on bilingual term alignment in specialised comparable corpora.

The aim of the workshop ConTeNTS 2023 is to promote new insights into the ongoing and forthcoming developments in computational terminology by bringing together NLP experts, as well as terminologists and translators. By uniting researchers with such diverse profiles, we hope to bridge some of the gaps between these disciplines and inspire a dialogue between various parties, thus paving the way to more artificial intelligence applications based on mutual collaboration between language and technology.

Every submission to the workshop was evaluated by at least two reviewers who were members of the Programme Committee.

The conference contributions were authored by a total of 12 scholars from 8 different countries: Algeria, Argentine, Bangladesh, Belgium, Bulgaria, Chile, Italy, Serbia, Turkey and United States. These figures attest to the international nature of the workshop.

We would like to thank all the colleagues who submitted papers to ConTeNTs 2023 and to BUCC 2023, and who travelled to Varna to attend the event, or presented their work online. We are also grateful to all members of the Programme Committee for providing constructive feedback on each paper. A special thanks goes to Reinhard Rapp, and to the invited Keynote speakers, namely Mo El-Haj from the Lancaster University and Sida I. Wang from Facebook AI Research (FAIR).

September 2023

Amal Haddad Haddad
Ayla Rigouts Terryn
Ruslan Mitkov

ConTeNTS:

Organising Committee & Workshop Chairs:

Amal Haddad Haddad (Universidad de Granada, Spain)
Ayla Rigouts Terryn (Katholieke Universiteit Leuven (KULAK) Belgium)
Ruslan Mitkov (Lancaster University, UK)

Programme Committee:

Sophia Ananiadou (University of Manchester)
Maria Andreeva Todorova (Bulgarian Academy of Sciences)
Silvia Bernardini (University of Bologna)
Melania Cabezas García (Universidad de Granada)
Esther Castillo Pérez (Universidad de Granada)
Rute Costa (Universidade Nova de Lisboa)
Patrick Drouin (Université de Montréal)
Pamela Faber (Universidad de Granada)
Mercedes García de Quesada (Universidad de Granada)
Dagmar Gromann (Centre for Translation Studies – University of Vienna)
Tran Thi Hong Hanh (L3i Laboratory, University of La Rochelle)
Rejwanul Haque (National College of Ireland)
Amir Hazem (Nantes University)
Milos Jakubicek (Lexical Computing)
Kyo Kageura (University of Tokyo)
Barbara Karsch (NYU)
Dorothy Kenny (Dublin City University)
Hendrik Kockaert (KU Leuven)
Philipp Koehn (Johns Hopkins University)
Maria Kunilovskaya (Saarland University)
Marie-Claude L'Homme (Université de Montréal)
Hélène Ledouble (Université de Toulon)
Pilar León-Araúz (Universidad de Granada)
Rodolfo Maslias (former Head of TermCoord, European Parliament)
Silvia Montero Martínez (Universidad de Granada)
Emmanuel Morin (LS2N-TALN)

Rogelio Nazar (Pontificia Universidad Católica de Valparaíso)
Sandrine Peraldi (University College Dublin)
Silvia Piccini (Italian National Research Council)
Thierry Poibeau (CNRS)
Senja Pollak (Jožef Stefan Institute)
Maria Pozzi Pardo (El Colegio de México)
Tharindu Ranasinghe (Aston University)
Arianne Reimerink (Universidad de Granada)
Andres Repar (Jožef Stefan Institute)
Christophe Roche (Université Savoie Mont-Blanc)
Antonio San Martín Pizarro (Université du Québec à Trois-Rivières)
Beatriz Sánchez Cárdenas (Universidad de Granada)
Vilelmini Sosoni (Ionian University)
Irena Spasic (Cardiff University)
Elena Isabelle Tamba (Romanian Academy, Iași Branch)
Rita Temmerman (Vrije Universiteit Brussel)
Jorge Vivaldi Palatresi (Universitat Pompeu Fabra)

BUCC:

Workshop Chairs:

Reinhard Rapp (Magdeburg-Stendal University of Applied Sciences and University of Mainz, Germany) Pierre Zweigenbaum, (Université Paris-Saclay, CNRS, LISN, Orsay, France) Serge Sharoff (University of Leeds, UK)

Programme Committee:

Ebrahim Ansari (Institute for Advanced Studies in Basic Sciences, Iran)
Thierry Etchegoyhen (Vicomtech, Spain)
Philippe Langlais (Université de Montréal, Canada)
Yves Lepage (Waseda University, Japan)
Shervin Malmasi (Amazon, USA)
Emmanuel Morin (Nantes Université, France)
Dragos Stefan Munteanu (Language Weaver, Inc., USA)
Reinhard Rapp (University of Mainz and Magdeburg-Stendal University of Applied Sciences, Germany)
Nasredine Semmar (CEA LIST, Paris, France)
Serge Sharoff (University of Leeds, UK)
Richard Sproat (OGI School of Science and Technology, USA)
Tim Van de Cruys (KU Leuven, Belgium)
Pierre Zweigenbaum (Université Paris-Saclay, CNRS, LISN, Orsay, France)

Table of Contents

Bilingual Terminology Alignment Using Contextualized Embeddings

Setha Imene
Research Center on Scientific
and Technical Information CERIST.
Algiers. Algeria
sethaimene1@gmail.com

Aliane Hassina
Research Center on Scientific
and Technical Information CERIST.
Algiers. Algeria
ahassina4@gmail.com

Abstract

Terminology Alignment faces big challenges in NLP because of the dynamic nature of terms. Fortunately, over these last few years, Deep Learning models have shown very good progress with several NLP tasks such as multilingual data resourcing, glossary building, terminology understanding...etc. In this work, we propose a new method for terminology alignment from a comparable corpus (Arabic/French languages) for the Algerian culture field.

We aim to improve bilingual alignment based on contextual information of a term and to create a significant term bank i.e. a bilingual Arabic-French dictionary. We propose to create word embeddings for both Arabic and French languages using ELMO model focusing on contextual features of terms. Then, we map those embeddings using a Seq2seq model.

We use multilingual-BERT and All-MiniLM-L6 as baseline models to compare terminology alignment results. Experimentations showed quite satisfying alignment results.

1 Introduction

For many years now, humans have wanted to enhance the machine's learning and understanding capacity to reach our potential of thinking, awareness, and power of judgment. making us wonder, is it close enough for a machine to be able to recognize and realize as we do? In artificial intelligence and NLP tasks, new models are frequently created to automate and facilitate life in different areas.

However, some fields have a long road to go, such as cross-lingual alignment and contextual translation. Terminology alignment is a very tough task to handle in NLP since one term can have several meanings according to its position and use. Aligned terms are often incorrect or misplaced especially while working with non-similar language families. For example, a sentence or a term might be translated into 3 or more different expressions and still not have the correct corresponding meaning. We can define bilingual terminology alignment as the process of mapping two terms or sentences in two different languages. Alignment provides significant benefits in many NLP tasks when properly applied like machine translation, clustering, building bilingual dictionaries, multilingual data resourcing...etc. The primary purpose of this work is to build a bilingual term bank for Arabic and French languages. Bilingual Alignment can be applied either to sentences or terms, in this article, we focus on bilingual terms only. According to (Och and Ney, 2003), we have a source language sentence containing the terms:

$$f = f1, f2, ...fj.$$

and a target language sentence:

$$e = e1, e2, \ldots ei.$$

An alignment A is defined as a subset of the Cartesian product of the word positions(Mikolov et al., 2013).

$$A \subseteq (j, i) : j = 1, ..., J; i = 1, ..., I$$

As shown in this example (See Figure 1):

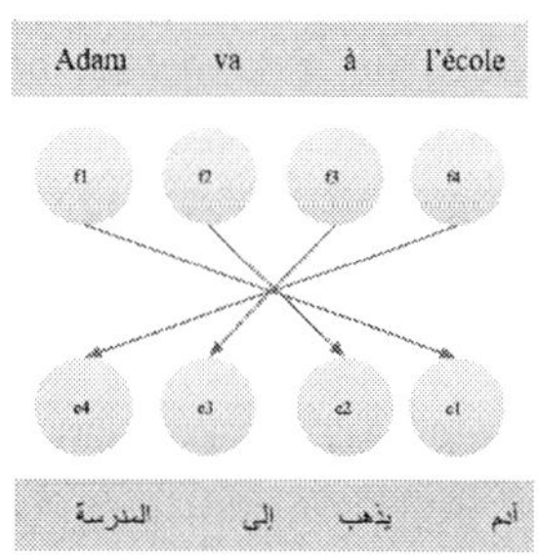

Figure 1: example of aligned terms in two languages

Proceedings of the First ConTenNTS Workshop and the 16th BUCC workshop, pages 1–8
Varna, Sep 7, 2023
https://doi.org/10.26615/978-954-452-090-8_001

The remainder of this paper is organized as follows. In section 2, we present related works on bilingual terminology alignment. Section 3 presents our methodology and system architecture. section 4 is dedicated to experiments and results of our method. We conclude the paper with a general conclusion and future perspectives.

2 Related Work

Although bilingual terminology alignment (referred to as BTA in the rest of the paper) task is challenging and tough, considerable efforts have been invested into this research field starting in the early 90s by IBM Watson research center (Brown et al., 1990) who introduced statistical alignment models, called IBM models using parallel corpora. Basically, there are 5 basic statistical models (IBM models, 2023) IBM1,2,3,4,5. Another one was added later combining IBM4 and HMM model(Hidden Markov model) based on assumptions such as:

- The target sentence length j is independent of source length i.
- For each target word, all alignments (including alignment to NULL) are equally likely and do not depend on the particular word or its position in the sentence.
- Once the alignments have been determined, the target word depends only on the source word to which it is aligned.
- The translation depends only on the source and target word pair, and not on any previous source or target words.
- The reordering depends only on the position of the target word, the position of the source word, and the lengths of the two sentences.

Many existing methods use IBM models, (Lee et al., 2010) applied IBM1 model using an unsupervised EM-based hybrid model[1] to extract bilingual terminology from comparable corpora through document alignment constraints. Using Giza++, (Moore, 2005) aligned their parallel corpus using the IBM4 model. As in (Macken et al., 2013) the famous TExSIS tool for terminology extraction is based on the IBM4 model for alignment. A combination of IBM1, IBM4 and HMM models is introduced in (Zhao and Xing, 2007) to perform alignment on parallel sentence pairs.

Besides IBM models, alternative statistical models focus on carried statistical properties of a given term or sentence, they vary from length-based, frequency-based, and lexical-based models. In (Salameh et al., 2011), the authors build a system to align English-Arabic sentences using a parallel corpus and focus on applying the best preprocessing steps to enhance their results. (Ittycheriah and Roukos, 2005) describes a maximum entropy-based method for Arabic-English term alignment. However, the recent state-of-the-art is basically governed by machine learning and deep learning models.

Generally, machine learning models treat alignment as a classification problem. In (Repar et al., 2018), the authors use an SVM model as a classifier for the task, adding some improvements to the model that was applied to the English-Slovinian language pair and applied to the Eurovoc thesaurus as the main dataset. (Kontonatsios et al., 2014) built a comparable corpus collected from Wikipedia as a 4k biomedical English term. The authors used a Logistic regression classifier for learning a string similarity measure of term translations. More recently, Deep Learning models achieved high scores and outstanding performance in understanding and translating words and phrases. A very interesting work by (Adjali et al., 2022) adopts the Compositional with Word Embedding Projection (CMWEP) approach of (Liu et al., 2018) to create dictionaries using a comparable corpus. They create WE's using FasText and learn the mapping using a linear transformation approach (Artetxe et al., 2016). (Dev et al., 2021) develop a family of techniques to align WEs, using several mechanisms such as glove, Word2Vec, and fastText, with Wikipedia as an initial dataset. In (Cao et al., 2020), the authors use multilingual BERT to align Bulgarian and Greek using a small parallel corpus extracted from Wikipedia. Another interesting work is (Garg et al., 2019) where the authors train a transformer and build an encoder-decoder model to build a framework for different language translations and where results outperform both Giza++ and IBM models results.

3 Proposed Approach

In this section, we describe our methods and models for BTA using context-based embeddings for both Arabic and French languages. We begin with

[1]Expectation Maximization model.

a system design that briefly shows the main used models and techniques for creating bilingual term pairs. starting with creating contextual WE to find the best equivalent of a given term from the source S to the target T language.

3.1 System Design

Our system depicted in Figure 2, involves the following steps:
Step1: create word vectors (the vocabulary) using the ELMO model for both source and target languages.
Step2: use a small dictionary to feed the models.
Step3: learn the alignments using a Seq2seq model.
Step4: align the list of terms from source to target languages.

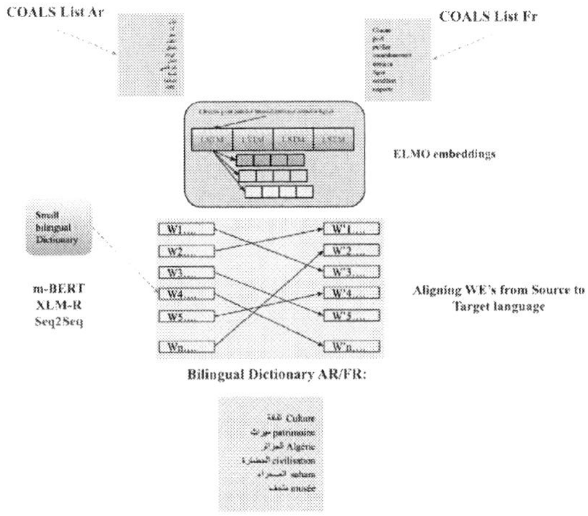

Figure 2: A global overview of the general system's architecture

3.2 Contextual Word Embeddings

Word embeddings (WE) are high-dimensional vector representations of words, based on the words' contexts. WE provide relevant, meaningful information for NLP tasks. The approaches for learning embeddings evolved from static free-word-order to contextualized and deeply contextualized. Word2Vec and Glove are context-independent, word-based representations that do not take word order into account in their training; for each word, we have just one vector as an output. This vector gathers all the meanings of the word. Elmo and BERT are contextual representations that take word order into account and can generate different vectors for a word, capturing all senses based on that word's position in the sentence. Our main goal is to capture the semantic features of a term, in order to compare term vectors across different languages. Therefore we chose Elmo to create our word embeddings WE.

3.3 ELMO

Contextual WE have been developed for better language modeling and to overcome the limitations of traditional methods. Elmo (Embedding for Language Models) (Gardner et al., 2018) has been developed by the Allen Institute NLP group. It is a bidirectional LSTM character-based model that learns word representations using character convolutions and can handle different vocabulary meanings. The main idea is to check all the sentences before creating the word vector, ELMO focuses only on the semantic features of terms, which makes ELMO highly relevant for the BTA task. Furthermore, the concatenation of right-to-left and left-to-right using LSTM should, in theory, generate more accurate word representations and therefore a better term alignment. In our work, we choose to use the Multilingual Elmo embeddings[2], which was pre-trained on 20 million words data randomly sampled from the raw text released by the shared task wiki dump + common crawl, (github, 2020) for 44 languages till this day.

3.4 Baseline Models

In order to evaluate our ELMO model, we have chosen to implement as baselines, recent models that have been successfully used in machine translation: Multilingual-Bert, All-MiniLM-L6, and Seq2seq combined with fasttext embeddings.

3.4.1 BERT-Base-Multilingual-Cased

Multilingual BERT (referred to as mBERT in the rest of the article) is an extension of the original BERT (Bidirectional Encoder Representations from Transformers) model. In other words, it is a multilingual version of BERT. BERT (Devlin et al., 2018) is the most powerful tool for language understanding in human history, and it is everywhere: e-mails, web pages, browsers...etc. It is an attention-based model that uses a transformer with positional encoding to represent word positions using a masked language modeling (MLM) objective.

[2]https://github.com/HIT-SCIR/ELMoForManyLangs

The transformer comprises an encoder to read the sentence and a decoder to predict the next lines. This means that BERT captures the context on both the left and right sides of the sentence to make a prediction. The main architecture comprises 12 layers(transformer blocks), 12 attention heads, and 110 million parameters (See Figure 3). The Google

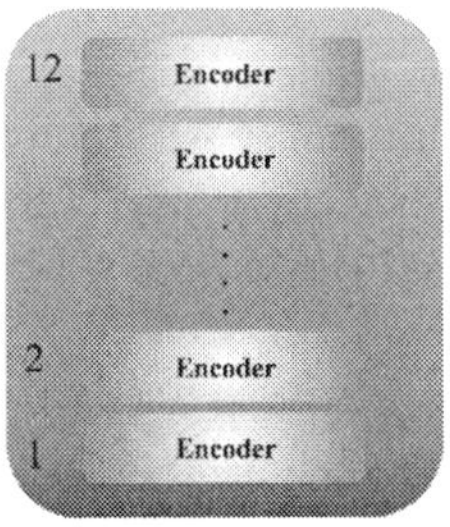

Figure 3: BERT's model general architecture

research team introduced mBERT (Devlin et al., 2018) very soon after the original BERT. It was initially pre-trained for 104 languages and it showed a great performance in several NLP tasks.

3.4.2 Seq2Seq Model With Fastext

Sequence to Sequence is a well-known machine translation model that was introduced by Google, it takes a sequence of items as inputs (terms, phrases, numbers…etc) and outputs another sequence of predicted items as well.(analyticsvidhya, 2023) Seq2Seq models use a powerful encoder-decoder neural mechanism, which is often based on Recurrent neural networks RNN (See Figure 4). Encoders read the input sequence and summarize the information in context vectors. We discard the outputs of the encoder by only preserving these vectors. Where context vectors aim to encapsulate the information for all input elements in order to help the decoder make accurate predictions(analyticsvidhya, 2023).

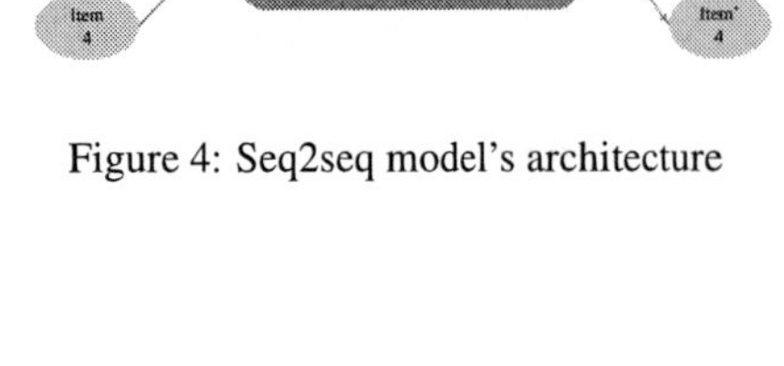

Figure 4: Seq2seq model's architecture

3.4.3 All-MiniLM-L6

All-MiniLM-L6 is a sentence transformer model that maps sentences and paragraphs to a 384-dimensional dense vector space and can be used for tasks like clustering or semantic search (huggingface, 2023). The model was pretrained on a 1B sentence pairs dataset using a contrastive learning objective: given a sentence from the pair, the model should predict which out of a set of randomly sampled other sentences, was actually paired with it in the dataset. This model is intended to be used as a sentence and short paragraph encoder. Given an input text, it outputs a vector that captures the semantic information. The sentence vector may be used for information retrieval, clustering, or sentence similarity tasks (huggingface, 2023)

4 Experiments & Results

In this section, we examine the performance of the baseline models for French and Arabic languages based on two tests. First, we start by using WEs in Seq2seq model with fasttext embeddings to compare WEs without contextual information with ELMO's embeddings for the mapping results. In the second experiment, we compare baseline models' results for the BTA task. Lastly, we evaluate the model's performance using evaluation metrics: Precision, Recall, and F1-score.

4.1 Dataset Resources

The main dataset of this work is provided from (Imene and Hassina, 2022) where a set of terms in Arabic and French languages were collected from Wikipedia pages in the "Algerian culture" domain pages and all related pages. Extracted pages went through a monolingual terminology extraction process using **COALS model** (Correlated Occurrence Analogue to Lexical Semantics)(Rohde et al., 2006). As we can see in Table 1, we use about 28k of Arabic tokens and 30k of French.

Terms language	Terms number
Arabic language	27 500 terms
French language	30 000 terms

Table 1: Dataset details.

4.2 Some Notes About The Dataset:

- The dataset contains 57 500K terms.

- We consider both simple and Muti-word terms for the process.
- Most of the Extracted terms are in-domain terms for the specific field of "Algerian culture" (See Figure 5).
- We feed some in-domain Multi-word terms into the dictionary to be recognized by the models.
- No preprocessing is applied, the vocabulary is already preprocessed in the terminology extraction step.

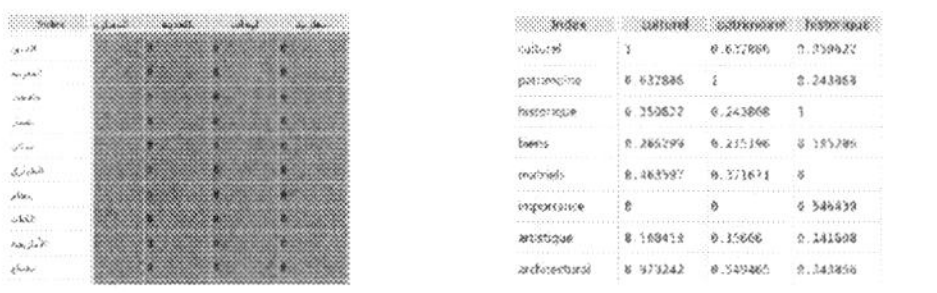

Figure 5: The general form of the dataset in French and Arabic languages

4.3 Seed Dictionary

We use our dataset to create a small dictionary. it contains about 200 terms matched with their exact equivalent from source to target language. We manually review the dictionary pairs to confirm all mapped terms. It contains both single-word and multi-word terms. We also try to add a sufficient number of Multi-word in-domain terms, and acronyms to better feed the alignment models. for example:

ONU → هيئة الأمم المتحدة
unicef → منظمة اليونيسيف
unesco → منظمة اليونسكو

This small bilingual dictionary is used as an additional resource to feed the models with some in-domain terms.

4.4 Evaluation Metrics

According to (Sabet et al., 2020), given a set of predicted alignment edges A and a set of sure, possible gold standard edges S, P (where S is a subset of P).
We use the following evaluation measures:

$$Recall = |A \cap S||S|$$

$$Precision : |A \cap P||A|$$

$$F1 - Score = (2PrecRec)/(Prec + Rec)$$

4.5 Contextual Space Vectors

Using the Elmo model, we create WE for source and target languages. Based on contextual features provided by the Elmo model, for instance, the term "patrimoine" and its translation conceivably share the same vector's structure as shown in Figure 6 below:

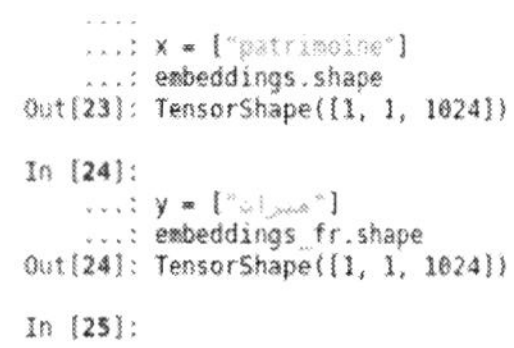

Figure 6: An example of two terms sharing the same WEs

- After finishing all previous steps we load the WE to apply our alignment method next.
- For the following tests we consider French as the source language and Arabic as the target language.
- We use Fasttext aligned monolingual vectors[3] to test with. The Facebook team provides these vectors in 89 languages and 78 aligned matrices including French and Arabic. Those matrices are aligned based on a linear transformation (matrix) using the SVD function.(Smith et al., 2017)

For the first test, we apply term alignment using the Seq2seq model with Elmo WE and Fasttext WE to compare them. We start by creating WEs using Elmo for our list of terms, then we use Fasttext vectors as well (We download the available multilingual space vectors for both Arabic and French).

Word vectors	Fasttext	ELMO
Alignment Precision on 100 terms of data	49.9%	62.3%

Table 2: Alignment results using Elmo & Fast-text

[3]https://github.com/facebookresearch/fastText

4.6 Alignment Process

In the upcoming experiments, we use a Desktop Computer with an Intel Core I5 7400 CPU with a 3.00 GHz frequency and 16 GB RAM. We also train our models on a workstation that contains 4 GPU RTX2080ti. We implement the proposed models using Python. Pytorch, tensorflow, and transformers libraries are used in the following experiments.

4.6.1 Multilingual-Bert

Multilingual Bert is a pre-trained model on 104 Wikipedia for 104 languages. Trained with 12 transformer layers, with 12 heads and 768 hidden dimensions each with a total number of 110M parameters. It scores high precision for translation tasks that reached 82% in English and 71% in Arabic. We load the model and apply it directly to our term's list, results are shown in Table 4.

4.6.2 Seq2Seq Model With Fasttext

Our second baseline model has been used for machine translation since 2014. We upload our Fasttext WEs, then we pass directly to create the RNN encoder-decoder networks using the Pytorch library. We train the model on 30 epochs to predict our list of Arabic terms.

4.6.3 All-MiniLM-L6

From the various available multilingual models that are based on sentence transformers, we chose All-MiniLM-L6, to align our vector spaces which is known for its fast results and good quality in semantic similarity search. We use the "Sentence-transformers" library to align not sentences but parts of them, which are in our case simple terms from source to target languages.

m-BERT	Seq2Seq	All-Mini-ML-6
le patrimoine = التراث	le patrimoine = ميراث	le patrimoine = التراث
Algérien = الجزائري	Algérien =جزائري	Algérien = الجزائري
la culture = الثقافة	la culture = الثقافة	la culture = الثقافة
la civilisation = الحضارة	la civilisation = الحضارة	la civilisation = الحضارة

Table 3: Alignment results from French to Arabic.

- Table 3 shows alignment results for the following terms respectfully: "patrimony", "Algerian" "Culture", and "civilization" (in French and Arabic languages).

4.7 Baselines Comparison

We compare previous baseline models to each other. We apply our test on the 100 first terms of both lists. to compare results between the models.

Alignment	Precision	Recall	F1-Score
M-BERT	84%	72%	77.5%
Seq2seq/Fasttext	50%	34%	40%
Seq2seq/ELMO	62%	46%	52.8%
All-MiniLM-L6	82%	70%	75.5%

Table 4: Evaluation results from French into Arabic.

4.8 Discussion

In this work, we tackle terminology alignment based on contextualized embeddings for a French/Arabic list of terms. We use three baseline models to apply the alignment. From the first experiment, we hypothesized that contextual embeddings would give better results in terminology alignment, which has shown to be true since Elmo's embeddings capture all meanings of terms and present it as a multiple vector choice to be aligned and Table 2 along with Figure 6 clearly confirms our hypothesis. In the second experiment, we align Arabic and French extracted terms using the proposed baseline models. Although Sentence transformer models are made to work mainly with phrases and paragraphs, results of mBERT and All-MiniLM-L6 are very close and alike, many translations are the same in both models and as shown in Table 3, we can see in the example of "civilization" term "la civilisation = "الحضارة" in mBERT while in All-MiniLM-L6 it means "حضارة".

The reason that those models perform better and give efficient results is related to the fact that the transformer's self-attention mechanism identifies the context which gives meaning to each position in the input sequence, allowing more parallelization than RNN models and reducing the training time. As for the Seq2seq model, we know that it is dedicated properly for long sequences i.e. paragraphs and sentences, however, the recurrent layer processes the input data in sequential order. These RNNs do not capture term position or order in the sentence which leads to a low term translation quality. Even So, our dataset is a comparable list of terms while the seq2seq model works better with parallel data. Overall, the manual comparison analysis we made for 100 first-aligned terms (See

Table 3) shows that transformer-based models are clearly the best choice for contextual terminology alignment. Therefore, mBERT and All-Mini-ML-6 score the highest precision(See Table 4).

5 Conclusion

In this paper, the new trending models in terminology alignment and machine translation are presented to improve the quality of alignment for several languages, especially Arabic. We chose to focus on the contextual angle of terminology alignment, to improve alignment quality. We use the ELMO model to create contextual Word vectors in order to capture terms' diversity of meaning, then use the Seq2seq model to align those vectors. We believe that the use of contextual word vectors might have a real impact on the alignment quality. We use mBERT, Seq2Seq(fast-text), and All-MiniLM-L6 Models to compare with our proposed method. Although mBERT outperforms all the models in our experiments, the results are very satisfying for the other models as well. Therefore, we think that the model we use in bilingual mapping should depend on the data size, data quality, and model parameters. In terms of future works, we are longing to create new aligned term banks, and dictionaries for other languages. We also hope to apply new models with new features to enhance the alignment quality.

References

Omar Adjali, Emmanuel Morin, and Pierre Zweigenbaum. 2022. Building comparable corpora for assessing multi-word term alignment. In *LREC 2022-Language Resources and Evaluation Conference*, pages 3103–3112.

analyticsvidhya. 2023. a simple introduction to sequence-to-sequence models. `https://huggingface.co/sentence-transformers/all-MiniLM-L6-v2`,.

Mikel Artetxe, Gorka Labaka, and Eneko Agirre. 2016. Learning principled bilingual mappings of word embeddings while preserving monolingual invariance. In *Proceedings of the 2016 conference on empirical methods in natural language processing*, pages 2289–2294.

Peter F Brown, John Cocke, Stephen A Della Pietra, Vincent J Della Pietra, Frederick Jelinek, John Lafferty, Robert L Mercer, and Paul S Roossin. 1990. A statistical approach to machine translation. *Computational linguistics*, 16(2):79–85.

Steven Cao, Nikita Kitaev, and Dan Klein. 2020. Multilingual alignment of contextual word representations. *arXiv preprint arXiv:2002.03518*.

Sunipa Dev, Safia Hassan, and Jeff M Phillips. 2021. Closed form word embedding alignment. *Knowledge and Information Systems*, 63(3):565–588.

Jacob Devlin, Ming-Wei Chang, Kenton Lee, and Kristina Toutanova. 2018. Bert: Pre-training of deep bidirectional transformers for language understanding. *arXiv preprint arXiv:1810.04805*.

Matt Gardner, Joel Grus, Mark Neumann, Oyvind Tafjord, Pradeep Dasigi, Nelson Liu, Matthew Peters, Michael Schmitz, and Luke Zettlemoyer. 2018. Allennlp: A deep semantic natural language processing platform. *arXiv preprint arXiv:1803.07640*.

Sarthak Garg, Stephan Peitz, Udhyakumar Nallasamy, and Matthias Paulik. 2019. Jointly learning to align and translate with transformer models. *arXiv preprint arXiv:1909.02074*.

github. 2020. Elmoformanylangs. Https://github.com/HIT-SCIR/ELMoForManyLangs.

huggingface. 2023. sentence transformers all-minilm-l6-v2. `https://huggingface.co/sentence-transformers/all-MiniLM-L6-v2`,.

IBM models. 2023. Types of models. `https://www.ibm.com/docs/en/spss-modeler/18.1.0?topic=mining-types-models`,.

Setha Imene and Aliane Hassina. 2022. An unsupervised semantic model for arabic/french terminology extraction. In *Proceedings of International Conference on Emerging Technologies and Intelligent Systems: ICETIS 2021 Volume 2*, pages 49–59. Springer.

Abraham Ittycheriah and Salim Roukos. 2005. A maximum entropy word aligner for arabic-english machine translation. In *Proceedings of Human Language Technology Conference and Conference on Empirical Methods in Natural Language Processing*, pages 89–96.

Georgios Kontonatsios, Ioannis Korkontzelos, Jun'ichi Tsujii, and Sophia Ananiadou. 2014. Combining string and context similarity for bilingual term alignment from comparable corpora. In *Proceedings of the 2014 Conference on Empirical Methods in Natural Language Processing (EMNLP)*.

Lianhau Lee, Aiti Aw, Min Zhang, and Haizhou Li. 2010. Em-based hybrid model for bilingual terminology extraction from comparable corpora. In *Coling 2010: Posters*, pages 639–646.

Jingshu Liu, Emmanuel Morin, and Sebastián Peña Saldarriaga. 2018. Towards a unified framework for bilingual terminology extraction of single-word and multi-word terms. In *Proceedings of the 27th International Conference on Computational Linguistics*, pages 2855–2866.

Lieve Macken, Els Lefever, and Veronique Hoste. 2013. Texsis: Bilingual terminology extraction from parallel corpora using chunk-based alignment. *Terminology. International Journal of Theoretical and Applied Issues in Specialized Communication*, 19(1):1–30.

Tomas Mikolov, Kai Chen, Greg Corrado, and Jeffrey Dean. 2013. Efficient estimation of word representations in vector space. *arXiv preprint arXiv:1301.3781*.

Robert C Moore. 2005. A discriminative framework for bilingual word alignment. In *Proceedings of Human Language Technology Conference and Conference on Empirical Methods in Natural Language Processing*, pages 81–88.

Franz Josef Och and Hermann Ney. 2003. A systematic comparison of various statistical alignment models. *Computational linguistics*, 29(1):19–51.

Andraz Repar, Matej Martinc, and Senja Pollak. 2018. Machine learning approach to bilingual terminology alignment: Reimplementation and adaptation. In *4REAL 2018 Workshop on Replicability and Reproducibility of Research Results in Science and Technology of Language*, pages 1–8.

Douglas LT Rohde, Laura M Gonnerman, and David C Plaut. 2006. An improved model of semantic similarity based on lexical co-occurrence. *Communications of the ACM*, 8(627-633):116.

Masoud Jalili Sabet, Philipp Dufter, François Yvon, and Hinrich Schütze. 2020. Simalign: High quality word alignments without parallel training data using static and contextualized embeddings. *arXiv preprint arXiv:2004.08728*.

Mohammad Salameh, Rached Zantout, and Nashat Mansour. 2011. Improving the accuracy of english-arabic statistical sentence alignment. *Int. Arab J. Inf. Technol.*, 8(2):171–177.

Samuel L Smith, David HP Turban, Steven Hamblin, and Nils Y Hammerla. 2017. Offline bilingual word vectors, orthogonal transformations and the inverted softmax. *arXiv preprint arXiv:1702.03859*.

Bing Zhao and Eric Xing. 2007. Hm-bitam: Bilingual topic exploration, word alignment, and translation. *Advances in Neural Information Processing Systems*, 20.

Termout: a tool for the semi-automatic creation of term databases

Rogelio Nazar
Instituto de Literatura y Ciencias del Lenguaje
Pontificia Universidad Católica de Valparaíso
rogelio.nazar@pucv.cl

Nicolás Acosta
Facultad de Filosofía y Letras
Universidad Nacional de Cuyo
niacosta@ms.uncu.edu.ar

Abstract

We propose a tool for the semi-automatic production of terminological databases, divided in the steps of corpus processing, terminology extraction, database population and management. With this tool it is possible to obtain a draft macrostructure (a lemma-list) and data for the microstructural level, such as grammatical (morphosyntactic patterns, gender, formation process) and semantic information (hypernyms, equivalence in another language, definitions and synonyms). In this paper we offer an overall description of the software and an evaluation of its performance, for which we used a linguistics corpus in English and Spanish.

1 Introduction

Terminology-related software has been available for more than sixty years (Hutchins, 1998), first promoted by the Vienna School (Wüster, 1979; Felber, 1984), but later gravitating towards computational linguistics (Sager, 1990; Kageura, 2012). Currently, the field of computer assisted terminology consists of a large variety of tools and methods, not only for term management (Steurs et al., 2015), but also for terminology extraction (Kageura and Umino, 1996; Rigouts Terryn et al., 2022), bilingual terminology alignment (Simões and Almeida, 2008; Filippova et al., 2021) and information extraction (Pearson, 1998; Meyer, 2001), among other related areas.

Despite all the efforts, there is still ample room for improvement not only in each of the individual areas but in the field as a whole. There is, in fact, no tool yet available that can offer an integral solution for all the different problems terminologists face up to when creating terminological databases. In this context, we present Termout[1], a tool for automatising, at least partially, many of those tasks.

[1] http://www.termout.org

The tool we present allows the user to process a specialised corpus and extract a draft macrostructure (a lemma-list) as well as data for the microstructural level, such as grammatical and semantic information. The possibilities of this software are very diverse and there is potential to benefit different professionals, foremost terminologists and lexicographers. Users are able to generate raw material which they can later improve manually by adding or correcting data. If the raw material is of some quality, it is undoubtedly better to build from it than starting from scratch. It is hoped that, with the help of this system, larger databases will be possible, saving time otherwise spent in tedious mechanical tasks.

The current implementation of the software is a web-based prototype that can perform the tasks of corpus processing (file uploading, conversion to plain-text format, language detection, POS-tagging and indexing), terminology extraction (with optional human supervision), information extraction (hypernymy, definitions, equivalence in another language, term variation, etc.) and database management (editing, storage, retrieval and import/export options in HTML, CSV and TBX).

In this paper we focus on the evaluation of the results of the main functions of the software: terminology and information extraction. To this end, we experimented with a linguistics corpus in English and Spanish. As the evaluation shows, in its current state the software can already be useful for terminology processing.

The structure of the paper is as follows. Section 2 offers a brief overview of computational terminology techniques with emphasis in terminology extraction. In Section 3 we present a description of the proposed method. Finally, in Section 4 we discuss about the advantages and disadvantages of the method as well as the challenges ahead.

Proceedings of the First ConTenNTS Workshop and the 16th BUCC workshop, pages 9–18
Varna, Sep 7, 2023
https://doi.org/10.26615/978-954-452-090-8_002

2 Related work

As mentioned in the introduction, the first efforts in initiating the computational treatment of terminology were by members of the Vienna School, but then the field took a turn towards empiricism and began to import methods from computational linguistics (Sager, 1990; Kageura, 2012). This change was accompanied by the emergence of new schools and theories, since data analysis lead to the admission of previously unrecognised phenomena, such as polysemy and term variation, which are less evident when relying only on introspection (Humbley, 2022).

Automatic terminology extraction (ATE), i.e. the separation of terms from the general vocabulary of a corpus (Kageura and Umino, 1996), was an early and strong force of change in practical terminology. The topic attracted the attention of many researchers and a wide variety of ideas were proposed. In the early years, some systems used statistical measures to detect multi-word terms (Daille, 1994; Frantzi et al., 2000). Others incorporated syntactic knowledge (Justeson and Katz, 1995; Bourigault et al., 1996). Others used statistics to calculate keywordness or weirdness, which means exploiting reference corpora by comparing the frequency of a term in a specialised corpus versus a corpus of general language (Ahmad et al., 1999; Drouin, 2003; Baisa et al., 2017).

The most recent tendency in the literature is the application of machine learning techniques, especially deep neural networks (Hazem et al., 2020; Lang et al., 2021; Rigouts Terryn et al., 2022; Tran et al., 2023). A drawback is however that their complexity makes them difficult to use, to interpret their results and, as Rigouts Terryn et al. (2020) point out, their behaviour is often unpredictable.

Aside from terminology extraction, other relevant subfields must be commented upon. One of those is bilingual terminology alignment using parallel, comparable or unrelated corpora (Simões and Almeida, 2008; Lefever et al., 2009; Aker et al., 2013; Haque et al., 2018; Filippova et al., 2021). Another subfield consists of the application of text mining techniques to obtain information about the terms from the corpus, which can be definitions (Pearson, 1998; Meyer, 2001; Anke et al., 2016); hypernymy relations (Hearst, 1992; Weeds and Weir, 2003; Bordea et al., 2015; Shwartz et al., 2017) and term variants (synonyms) (Ville-Ometz et al., 2007; Cram and Daille, 2016). The work by Wachowiak et al. (2021) is a recent example of a combination of term and term-relation extraction.

The number of relevant and recent publications to the different subareas of computer assisted terminology is on the thousands and still rising. However, the tendency seems to be analytical, i.e., to specialise in the different individual problems. As a consequence, not may proposals exist for the comprehensive solutions needed in practical terminology. There are some terminology extraction services (e.g. OneClick Terms[2] or MultiTerm[3]), but no software exists, commercial or public, that can accompany the user in the different steps of a terminology project. The software Terminus[4] (Cabré and Nazar, 2011) was a first attempt in that direction, but it was not further developed.

The present year 2023 is, of course, one of unprecedented changes in the field of A.I., and it is likely that new proposals for terminology processing will come from that side. In fact, some lexicographers (de Schryver and Joffe, 2023) have already started using ChatGPT (OpenAI, 2023) to automate different lexicographic tasks. Again, the results of neural network algorithms using large language models are promising although unpredictable, as they occasionally "hallucinate"[5].

In this juncture, we still think that there is room for experimentation with alternative methods, especially if they do not entail great complexity, require massive computing power and are not own by large private corporations.

3 Description and evaluation of the prototype

3.1 Overview

The described tool is designed to help the terminologist in every step of a project. The routines for the development of a terminology database are the compilation and processing of a specialised corpus (3.2); terminology extraction (3.3), information extraction (3.4) and database management (3.5). In order to evaluate the different functions we compiled a corpus of research articles from 15 open access scientific journals in English and Spanish in

[2] https://terms.sketchengine.eu/

[3] https://www.trados.com/products/multiterm-desktop/

[4] http://terminus.iula.upf.edu/

[5] According to the technical report, "care should be taken when using the outputs of GPT-4, particularly in contexts where reliability is important" (OpenAI, 2023, p. 2).

the field of general linguistics[6]. The sample consists of 3680 PDF files with a total extension of ca. 35 million word tokens.

3.2 Corpus preprocessing

With this tool, a terminology project starts with a corpus, which at the moment must be provided by the user[7]. A specialised corpus (Pavel and Nolet, 2002; Steurs et al., 2015) must cover a single topic or domain, must have some authority in the field and, most importantly, it must be very large. The latter is especially important in our case, as results deteriorate considerably with corpus of less than 200 documents.

The corpus can be uploaded as a ZIP file. It will be uncompressed and each input document will be submitted to the following processes:

Format detection and conversion: The program will guess the type of file (ZIP, TXT, PDF, PS, DOC, DOCX, ODT, HTML, XML, etc.) and convert it to UTF-8 Unix plain text format.

Language detection: It detects the main language of each document and also fragments of text inside that are in a different language. This is based on text similarity measures using samples of text in different languages. The text samples were downloaded from the Wortschatz Project[8] (Goldhahn et al., 2012). The program will only accept text in the supported languages (for now, only English and Spanish).

POS-tagging: Once with the documents separated by language, the corpus is submitted to a POS-tagging procedure. This is done with UDPipe (Straka and Straková, 2017), an external tool.

Indexing: As the program makes intensive use of concordance extraction for various functions, speed is thus critical, and for this a corpus indexing is needed as part of the pre-processing. We developed an indexing method consisting of a table with the positions of each word type in the corpus.

[6] We downloaded papers published in the last 15 years in the following journals: Alfal (ISSN 2079-312X); Anuario de letras (2448-8224); Boletín de Lingüística (0798-9709); Colombian Applied Linguistics Journal (0123-4641); Cuadernos de Lingüística Hispánica (0121-053X); Forma y Función (0120-338X); Íkala (0123-3432); Lenguaje (0120-3479); Letras (0459-1283); Lexis (0254-9239); Lingüística (2079-312X); Literatura y lingüística (0716-5811); Logos (0716-7520); Núcleo (0798-9784); Signos (0718-0934) and RLA (0718-4883).

[7] New functions for automatic corpus compilation are now in development, as explained in Section 4.

[8] https://wortschatz.uni-leipzig.de

3.3 Terminology extraction

As explained in Section 2, terminology extraction is a categorisation problem in which, for every term candidate, a system will produce as a result a score which will lead to the acceptance or rejection of the candidate. In this respect, this system does not depart from traditional approaches, but the method to score the term candidates is original.

The proposed terminology extraction method has a battery of filters arranged in increasing order of computational complexity, finishing in a combination of statistical measures. The initial exclusion rules are computationally inexpensive because they are based on stoplists and morphosyntactic patterns. The core of the method is the later application of a series of statistical measures such as term frequency, dispersion (based on document frequency) and co-occurrence (the analysis of other words sharing the same sentences with the candidate).

The first step of the terminology extraction procedure is the creation of lists of word n-grams (with n defined by the user, ranging from 1 to 5 by default). Each n-gram is treated as a potential term and submitted to the following battery of measures:

Stoplist: This is a set of simple exclusion rules to eliminate $n$grams that begin or end with a member of a list of function words (grammemes such as prepositions, articles, conjunctions, some adverbs, etc.). These function words are however admitted inside the candidate, as it may occur with some $n$grams with $n > 2$ (e.g., the linguistics term *part of speech*).

Morphosyntactic patterns: In this project we have opted to limit the number of term candidates to those which can be parsed as noun phrases. Candidates including other grammatical categories or patterns, such as verbs or adverbs, are excluded[9].

Term frequency: For any candidate x that survives the previous filters, we calculate its term frequency: $f(x)$. This measure might not be useful in isolation or while analysing a single document, as most terms in a text will be hapax legomena or dis legomena, but it can be a useful indicator if used in conjunction with other statistical measures and when analysing a large collection of specialised documents.

Dispersion: This measure is defined as a combination of term frequency and document frequency,

[9] This is certainly a limitation for users interested in specialised predicates, but these units may require a different methodology.

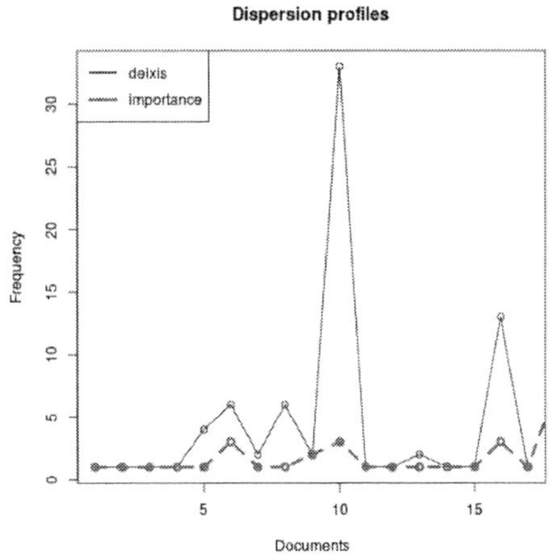

Figure 1: Dispersion of units *deixis*, a linguistics term, and *importance*, a non-term, in a sample of documents

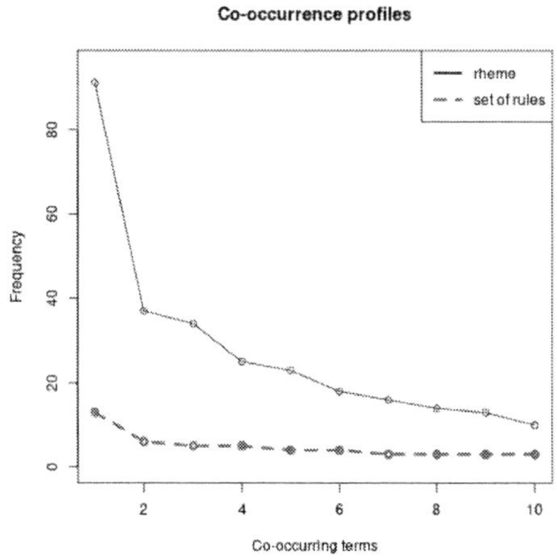

Figure 2: Co-occurrence profile of units *rheme*, a linguistics term, and *set of rules*, a non-term

$df(x)$, i.e. the number of documents in which a term occurs. When one observes how a candidate is distributed within a corpus, useful patterns begin to emerge, which can be exploited to make a prediction. Drawing inspiration from Spärck Jones (1972), we used coefficient (1) to measure the dispersion of a candidate. It can be described as a simplified derivative of tf-idf, less costly to compute. The variable $h(x)$ in (2) is the number of documents in a collection D in which term x has frequency 1.

$$d(x) = 1 - \frac{h(x)}{df(x)} \tag{1}$$

$$h(x) = \sum_{i=1}^{|D|} \begin{cases} 1 & f(x, D_i) = 1 \\ 0 & \text{otherwise} \end{cases} \tag{2}$$

Figure 1 shows the dispersion of two units in the corpus. The blue, continuous line corresponds to the term *deixis*, a genuine linguistics term, and the red, dashed line to *importance*, a non-term. Rough curves with sharp spikes appear to be associated with higher information, because they show that when a term occurs in a document, it is also likely that it will be used more than once. On the contrary, smoother curves mean that the expression is often used once per document, a pattern associated with non-terminological units.

Co-occurrence: As shown in previous work dating back from Harris (1954) and Firth (1957), one can know about a word by looking at the company it keeps. In this case, this means that terminological units are often revealed by their co-occurrence patterns, and this can be used as a robust predictor of the specialised value of a candidate. Terms show a tendency to co-occur with a reduced number of other terms which conform their semantic field. For instance, Figure 2 shows the case of a pair of units, *rheme*, a linguistics term (blue, continuous line), and *set of rules*, a sequence of words with no terminological value (red, dashed line). As expected, the term shows a tendency to appear in the same sentences with other related terms such as *theme, clause, progression, sentence*, etc. The other one, however, does not show a strong association with any other word despite being 20 times more frequent than the first. We used a co-occurrence measure (3) to exploit this phenomenon.

$$c(x) = \frac{\log_2 \sum_{i=1}^{k} R_{x,i}}{\log_2 f(x)} \tag{3}$$

In Equation 3, x is a term candidate; R_x the set of (single) words co-occurring with x; $f(x)$ is, again, the frequency of x and $R_{x,i}$ the frequency of the ith most frequent co-occurring word in the contexts of occurrence of x. The value k is an arbitrary parameter[10].

Extras: With variable $e(x)$ we denote an additional value for x when it is found in the title of bibliographic references in the corpus and/or when definitional patterns are found in the immediate vicinity of a term (the program includes a module

[10] In our experiments, $k = 20$. Larger ks mean longer processing times, but not necessarily better results. Users will have to experiment and adjust this parameter themselves to find the best compromise.

for the extraction of definitions from the corpus, explained later in Subsection 3.4). Appearing in titles and being defined are both taken as indicators of the significance of a term.

Final score: The above mentioned statistical measures, frequency, dispersion, co-occurrence and extras, defined as set A (4), are combined to produce a final score $s(x)$ (5). A threshold for this score is defined by the user.

$$A = \{\sqrt{f(x)}, d(x), c(x), e(x)\} \tag{4}$$

$$s(x) = \prod_{i=1}^{|A|}(1 + A_i) \tag{5}$$

After the calculations, the system also classifies the term candidates by language, which is done by inspecting the language of their contexts of occurrence, using the same mechanism described in 3.2. It also displays tables of rejected candidates that scored close to the cutting threshold, so users can manually rescue eventual false negatives. There is also the possibility of eliminating all candidates that include any arbitrary component.

As an alternative, the program also offers the user the possibility of uploading a list of terms to be used as examples. In this way, users may obtain more refined results, as the program will promote those candidates that tend to co-occur with those presented as examples. In particular, this last function may benefit those users who need terms of a very specific topic but only have a general corpus of the discipline (e.g., those interested only in phonology terms but having a general linguistics corpus or interested in PTSD terms but having a general psychiatry corpus, etc.).

For the purpose of evaluation, we extracted terms from the corpus restricting the minimum frequency to 10, a conservative parameter that favours precision over recall. This way we obtained a total of 1882 term candidates, automatically separated by language: 618 in English and 1264 in Spanish. The separation by language was almost perfect (we found only four errors). Regarding the term/non term separation, there were 104 false positives in English and 190 in Spanish. That makes a total precision of 84%.

Some examples of correct terms in English are the following: *argument structure; bilingualism; evidentiality; universal grammar*, etc. Among the errors we find some proper nouns (*Alarcos Llorach; Berkeley Linguistics Society; Prentice Hall*; etc.), some subject-verb pairs (*students work; teachers need*, etc.) among other cases (*assistant professor; Chinese student*, etc.). Figure 3 shows a screenshot of the program's interface with a fragment of the list of extracted candidates.

Figure 3: A screenshot of the results of the terminology extraction function

3.4 Information extraction

Once a list a terms has been obtained and, ideally, manually revised, the program then offers a battery of functions to populate the terminology database with a number of fields. Aside from fields such as inflection, grammatical gender and part of speech, the following functions provide further database enrichment:

Semantic categorisation: This function produces full hypernymy chains for each extracted term in each language, with progressive levels of abstraction and a graphic depiction of the conceptual hierarchies. The algorithm that produces this result combines co-occurrence statistics and morphosyntactic patterns (Nazar et al., 2021). Co-occurrence statistics tend to be asymmetric in the case of hyponym-hypernym pairs, in such a way that hyponyms show a tendency to co-occur with hypernyms in a non-reciprocal relation. This is combined with rules of morphosyntactic patterns *à la* Hearst (1992), which are used to triangulate information and reinforce a suspicion of hypernymy between pairs of terms. The main difference with respect to previous research using such type of patterns is that our algorithm only uses them to gather information about one term at a time. That is, it first collects all the contexts of occurrence of a given term and then computes statistics on the number of patterns found among those contexts.

An example of a correct result for the case of the term *articulatory phonetics* is the following hypernymy chain: *phonetics* → *linguistics* → *social science* → *science* → *study* → *abstract entity*

→ *entity*. After the evaluation, we found that in 99% of the cases there was a result and 64% of those were correct. The main cause of errors in the assignment of hypernym chains were cases of polysemy, in particular regular polysemy. An example of this type of error is the following: *narrative text → document → artefact → physical object*. The problem here is that the term *narrative text* in our corpus actually refers to the abstract content of the text, not the physical object.

Semantic clustering: This function produces clusters of terms that are semantically related. Here, a semantic relation is operationalised as co-occurrence associations computed as in Subsection 3.3, and the clustering is done with a co-occurrence-graph algorithm[11]. Specialised terms have a semantic field consisting of a set of other terms. Consequently, terms sharing a similar co-occurrence profile are placed in the same cluster.

For the evaluation of this function, a total of 65 clusters were produced, of which 83% presented internal consistency. For instance, one cluster presents discourse-related terms, another presents corpus linguistics terms, and so on. Figure 4 shows a fragment of a cluster the system creates with 35 terms in this case related to phonology in Spanish. For the visualisation of these graphs we used the GraphViz library (Gansner and North, 2000).

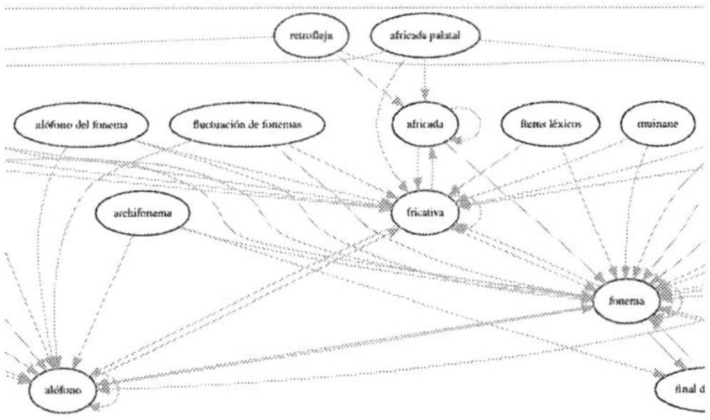

Figure 4: A fragment of a co-occurrence-graph cluster for phonology terms in Spanish

Spurious clusters were invariably cases with weakly interconnected nodes, and this could be exploited to further develop the method.

Definitions: With this function, users can obtain definitions of the terms from the corpus. For this we manually compiled a large list of definitional patterns in English and Spanish. Similarly as with the extraction of hypernymy chains, we first scan all the contexts of occurrence of a given term and extract the concordances that match a definitional pattern. These concordances are then sorted according the type of pattern found and its proximity to the analysed term.

For the evaluation we considered a correct result one in which for a term at least one context (out of max. 5) provides enough data for a definition. Consider, for instance, the following result for the case of *language planning*: "language planning refers to deliberate efforts to influence the behaviour of others with respect to the acquisition, structure, or functional allocation of language"[12]). Considering only the definitions extracted for the genuine terms, we found that 53% of the proposed definitions were acceptable; 12% of the cases produced no result and the rest were errors.

Bilingual alignment: Users can obtain a bilingual alignment of the extracted terms. This is achieved by applying a combination of dispersion and co-occurrence association measures, including also an orthographic similarity coefficient for the cognates. To calculate dispersion and co-occurrence we followed a similar principle as in Subsection 3.3. In the case of co-occurrence, the only difference is that in this case the interest is to find the intensity of the association between two terms i and j, for which we used coefficient 6. As in Subsection 3.3, this measures co-occurrence in the same sentences, irrespective of the order and distance between the two terms. In the case of dispersion and orthographic similarity, we used coefficient 7, in one case to measure how many documents two terms i and j have in common and in the other case how many character bigrams (sequences of two letters) they share.

$$coo(i,j) = \frac{f(i,j)}{\sqrt{f(i)}.\sqrt{f(j)}} \tag{6}$$

$$sim(i,j) = \frac{2|i \cap j|}{|i| + |j|} \tag{7}$$

Regarding the evaluation, from the sample of extracted terms we obtained 466 alignments (75% of the 618 English terms). Among these, we found a total of 108 errors (ca. 77% precision). Some example of correct alignments are the following: *academic genre = género académico; action verbs = verbos de acción; phonological system = sistema*

[11] We developed a clustering method based on co-occurrence graphs to avoid the quadratic complexity of to classical agglomerative clustering algorithms.

[12] The fragment is attributed to Cooper, R. L. (1989). Language Planning and Social Change. Cambridge University Press.

fonológico, etc. Typical errors are alignments of terms that are semantically related but not equivalent (e.g. *conceptual metaphor* $\neq$ *dominio fuente; critical language awareness* $\neq$ *conciencia crítica; foreign language learners* $\neq$ *lengua extranjera*). Figure 5 shows a moment of the bilingual alignment process.

Figure 5: Examples of bilingual alignment

Term variants: The final function in this Section consists of extracting term variants, i.e. terms in the same language which have different forms but the same meaning. In our case, the proposal to address this problem is based on the bilingual alignment conducted in the previous function, and it follows a simple intuition: two terms in the same language i and j can be considered term variants if they consistently share the same equivalences in the other language. For instance, *analyser* and *parser* are considered specialised synonyms because they share the same equivalence in Spanish (*analizador*), and the same occurs for other pairs such as *semantic field* $\sim$ *semantic space; coefficient* $\sim$ *ratio; discourse* $\sim$ *speech; poll* $\sim$ *survey; phrase* $\sim$ *sentence; core* $\sim$ *nucleus; meaning* $\sim$ *significance*; etc. Examples in Spanish are similar: *alfabetismo crítico* $\sim$ *alfabetización crítica; debate* $\sim$ *discusión; aplicación* $\sim$ *implementación*, and so on.

From the dataset of 1884 terms, a total of 105 pairs or groups of variant terms were obtained. From those, 60 cases we confirmed to be genuine synonyms (57%). Typical errors consist of pairs of words that are semantically related but are not synonyms (e.g. *learning* $\neq$ *pupil; apprenticeship* $\neq$ *learning; classroom* $\neq$ *teaching*, etc.).

Task	Precision
Term extraction	84%
Semantic categorisation	64%
Semantic clustering	83%
Definition extraction	53%
Bilingual alignment	77%
Term variant extraction	57%

Table 1: Summary of evaluation figures per task

3.5 Term management

In addition to the term extraction and information extraction functions, the tool also offers the possibility of manually editing the database in order to correct false information, to complete term records with missing data, or to delete and/or create new term records.

The system also offers the standard functions for querying the database with a search form that allows to retrieve information by any field or a combination of fields. As usual in this type of systems, a user may, for instance, retrieve all the terms that have a certain component (word or segment of word), or a certain term as a hypernym, or as equivalent, as synonym, etc.

When satisfied with the result, users can export the database in CSV, TBX or HTML formats. They can also import databases in CSV or in an industry standard such as TBX (Melby, 2015). The latter can be convenient for users already having a terminology database that needs to be completed, expanded or edited.

3.6 Summary of evaluation figures

Table 1 offers a summary of the evaluation figures obtained in this section, indicated in all cases as precision rates. Evaluation of recall for all functions would be harder to estimate in most cases. It would be possible to approximate a figure of recall in the case of term extraction by manually annotating some documents. But in the case of other functions it would be more challenging. Consider, for instance, the case of semantic clustering or bilingual alignment. It is difficult to determine how many clusters or alignments are in the corpus. We therefore leave the evaluation of recall for a future paper.

Here we also have to mention that some researchers have proposed annotated corpora to evaluate term extraction systems. Among them, we find the ACL RD-TEC 2.0 (QasemiZadeh and Schumann, 2016) and the TermEval 2020 (Rigouts Terryn et al., 2020). We did not use these materials, however, for different reasons. In the first case, because it is intended for systems that operate on the sentence-level, and thus they only include small fragments of text (abstracts). In contrast, our system is designed to work with natural, integral texts. In the second case, because we seem to have a different definition of what constitutes a term. As already mentioned, we only include sequences that can be parsed as noun phrases. We exclude predicate-argument structures as terminological units (e.g., for us, to *combat corruption* or *fight corruption* are not multi-word terms, but a combination of a verb and its complement).

4 Conclusions and future work

In this paper we presented a software for terminology processing that integrates a variety of tools for the creation of a terminology database, and we reported on a series of tests to evaluate its performance. As a first take after our assessment, we believe that despite some limitations, it could be useful for professional lexicographers and terminologists. In addition, we see also a possible application of the tool in the teaching of terminology, as students may use it to learn from practical experience in term database creation.

As pointed out in the introduction, there is today no single software product that can provide solutions for the different tasks involved in term-database creation. The software products now available for terminology and lexicography processing are too time-consuming. We believe, thus, that a tool such as the one we propose is useful not only for the convenience of automation but also because a technical glossary should be created using specialised corpora as input. Another advantage of the proposal is that it is based on simple algorithms, compared to those using neural networks. Dispersion and co-occurrence statistics can be performed in relatively cheap hardware, although it is still necessary to improve computational efficiency to reduce processing times.

The current implementation of Termout is freely available and has no restrictions of any kind. This might become a problem if the number of users increases significantly, since we lack the necessary infrastructure (manpower, servers, etc.). If confronted with such scenario, we would be forced to explore alternatives for sustainability.

It is also worth pointing out that the system uses no information external to the user's own corpus. We are, however, considering the possibility of changing this in future versions, in order to include the optional use of Wikipedia or other external knowledge sources.

Another point to mention is that, currently, the system only operates with English and Spanish text. However, the method is fundamentally based on statistical and language-agnostic algorithms, apart from the POS-tagger and the lexical patterns used in the extraction of hypernyms and definitions. We are, indeed, already attempting to adapt the system to different European languages.

We are also exploring new ways to let the users acquire corpora, and this function will soon be available. One alternative is to provide the program with a URL that contains links to other documents, and let the program decide which links are relevant. The other possibility is to upload a single document that the program will use to automatically extract, using text-similarity measures, a subset of similar documents from a larger general corpus such as the TenTen corpora collection (Jakubíček et al., 2013). This will offer the user the possibility of having the most laborious tasks of a terminology project fully automated.

Acknowledgments

This research received funding from a grant by the Chilean Government (Proyecto Fondecyt Regular 1231594, directed by Irene Renau). We would also like to thank the reviewers for their work.

References

Khurshid Ahmad, Lee Gillam, and Lena Tostevin. 1999. University of surrey participation in trec8: Weirdness indexing for logical document extrapolation and retrieval (wilder). In *TREC*, volume 500-246 of *NIST Special Publication*. National Institute of Standards and Technology (NIST).

Ahmet Aker, Monica Paramita, and Rob Gaizauskas. 2013. Extracting bilingual terminologies from comparable corpora. In *Proceedings of the 51st Annual Meeting of the Association for Computational Linguistics (Volume 1: Long Papers)*, pages 402–411, Sofia, Bulgaria. Association for Computational Linguistics.

Luis Espinosa Anke, Roberto Carlini, Horacio Saggion, and Francesco Ronzano. 2016. Defext: A semi supervised definition extraction tool. *CoRR*, abs/1606.02514.

Vít Baisa, Jan Michelfeit, and Ondřej Matuška. 2017. Simplifying terminology extraction: Oneclick terms. In *Proceedings of the 9th International Corpus Linguistics Conference*.

Georgeta Bordea, Paul Buitelaar, Stefano Faralli, and Roberto Navigli. 2015. Semeval-2015 task 17: Taxonomy extraction evaluation (texeval). In *Proceedings of the 9th International Workshop on Semantic Evaluation (SemEval 2015)*, pages 902–910, Denver, Colorado. Association for Computational Linguistics.

Didier Bourigault, Isabelle Gonzalez-Mullier, and Cécile Gros. 1996. Lexter, a natural language processing tool for terminology extraction. In *Proceedings of the 7th EURALEX International Congress*, pages 771–779, Göteborg, Sweden. Novum Grafiska AB.

Teresa Cabré and Rogelio Nazar. 2011. Terminus: a workstation for terminology and corpus management. In *Proceedings TOTh 2011*, pages 73–74. Presses Universitaires Savoie Mont Blanc.

Damien Cram and Béatrice Daille. 2016. Termsuite: Terminology extraction with term variant detection. In *54th Annual Meeting of the Association for Computational Linguistics, ACL 2016 - System Demonstrations*, pages 13–18.

Béatrice Daille. 1994. *Approche mixte pour l'extraction de terminologie : statistique lexicale et filtres linguistiques*. Ph.D. thesis. Paris 7.

Patrick Drouin. 2003. Term extraction using non-technical corpora as a point of leverage. *Terminology*, 9(1):99–115.

Helmut Felber. 1984. *Terminology manual*. United Nations Educational, Scientific and Cultural Organization : International Information Centre for Terminology, Paris.

Darya Filippova, Burcu Can, and Gloria Corpas Pastor. 2021. Bilingual terminology extraction using neural word embeddings on comparable corpora. In *Proceedings of the Student Research Workshop Associated with RANLP 2021*, pages 58–64.

John Firth. 1957. A synopsis of linguistic theory, 1930-55. In *Studies in Linguistic Analysis*, pages 1–31. Blackwell, Oxford.

Katerina Frantzi, Sophia Ananiadou, and Hideki Mima. 2000. Automatic recognition of multi-word terms:. the c-value/nc-value method. *International Journal on Digital Libraries*, 3(2):115–130.

Emden R. Gansner and Stephen C. North. 2000. An open graph visualization system and its applications to software engineering. *Softw. Pract. Exper.*, 30(11):1203–1233.

Dirk Goldhahn, Thomas Eckart, and Uwe Quasthoff. 2012. Building large monolingual dictionaries at the Leipzig corpora collection: From 100 to 200 languages. In *Proceedings of the Eighth International Conference on Language Resources and Evaluation (LREC'12)*, pages 759–765, Istanbul, Turkey. European Language Resources Association (ELRA).

Rejwanul Haque, Sergio Penkale, and Andy Way. 2018. Termfinder: log-likelihood comparison and phrase-based statistical machine translation models for bilingual terminology extraction. *Language Resources and Evaluation*, 52(2):365–400.

Zellig Harris. 1954. Distributional structure. *Word*, 10(2-3):146–162.

Amir Hazem, Mérieme Bouhandi, Florian Boudin, and Beatrice Daille. 2020. TermEval 2020: TALN-LS2N system for automatic term extraction. In *Proceedings of the 6th International Workshop on Computational Terminology*, pages 95–100, Marseille, France. European Language Resources Association.

Marti A. Hearst. 1992. Automatic acquisition of hyponyms from large text corpora. In *COLING 1992 Volume 2: The 14th International Conference on Computational Linguistics*.

John Humbley. 2022. The reception of Wüster's general theory of terminology. In Pamela Faber and Marie-Claude L'Homme, editors, *Theoretical Perspectives on Terminology. Explaining terms, concepts and specialized knowledge*, pages 15–36. John Benjamins, Amsterdam.

John Hutchins. 1998. The origins of the translator's workstation. *Machine Translation*, 13(4):287–307.

Miloš Jakubíček, Adam Kilgarriff, Vojtěch Kovář, Pavel Rychlý, and Vít Suchomel. 2013. The TenTen Corpus Family. In *7th International Corpus Linguistics Conference CL 2013*, pages 125–127, Lancaster.

John S. Justeson and Slava M. Katz. 1995. Technical terminology: some linguistic properties and an algorithm for identification in text. *Natural Language Engineering*, 1(1):9–27.

Kyo Kageura. 2012. *The Quantitative Analysis of the Dynamics and Structure of Terminologies*. John Benjamins.

Kyo Kageura and Bin Umino. 1996. Methods of automatic term recognition: A review. *Terminology*, 3(1):259–289.

Christian Lang, Lennart Wachowiak, Barbara Heinisch, and Dagmar Gromann. 2021. Transforming term extraction: Transformer-based approaches to multilingual term extraction across domains. In *Findings of the Association for Computational Linguistics: ACL-IJCNLP 2021*, pages 3607–3620. Association for Computational Linguistics.

Els Lefever, Lieve Macken, and Veronique Hoste. 2009. Language-independent bilingual terminology extraction from a multilingual parallel corpus. In *EACL 2009 - 12th Conference of the European Chapter of the Association for Computational Linguistics, Proceedings*, pages 496–504.

Alan Melby. 2015. TBX: A terminology exchange format for the translation and localization industry. In Hendrik Kockaert et al., editor, *Handbook of Terminology*, pages 393–424. John Benjamins, Amsterdam.

Ingrid Meyer. 2001. Extracting a knowledge-rich contexts for terminography: A conceptual and methodological framework. In D. Bourigault, C. Jaquemin, and M.C. L'Homme, editors, *Recent Advances in Computational Terminology*, pages 279–302. John Benjamins, Amsterdam.

Rogelio Nazar, Antonio Balvet, Gabriela Ferraro, Rafael Marín, and Irene Renau. 2021. Pruning and repopulating a lexical taxonomy: experiments in spanish, english and french. *Journal of Intelligent Systems*, 30(1):376–394.

OpenAI. 2023. Gpt-4 technical report.

Silvia Pavel and Diane Nolet. 2002. *Manual de Terminología.* Translation Bureau. Public Works and Government Services, Québec.

Jennifer Pearson. 1998. *Terms in Context.* John Benjamins, Amsterdam.

Behrang QasemiZadeh and Anne-Kathrin Schumann. 2016. The ACL RD-TEC 2.0: A language resource for evaluating term extraction and entity recognition methods. In *Proceedings of the Tenth International Conference on Language Resources and Evaluation (LREC'16)*, Portorož, Slovenia. European Language Resources Association (ELRA).

Ayla Rigouts Terryn, Veronique Hoste, Patrick Drouin, and Els Lefever. 2020. TermEval 2020: Shared task on automatic term extraction using the annotated corpora for term extraction research (ACTER) dataset. In *Proceedings of the 6th International Workshop on Computational Terminology*, pages 85–94, Marseille, France. European Language Resources Association.

Ayla Rigouts Terryn, Veronique Hoste, and Els Lefever. 2022. D-terminer : online demo for monolingual and bilingual automatic term extraction. In *Proceedings of the Workshop on Terminology in the 21st century*, pages 33–40. European Language Resources Association (ELRA).

Juan C. Sager. 1990. *A Practical Course in Terminology Processing.* John Benjamins, Amsterdam.

Gilles-Maurice de Schryver and David Joffe. 2023. The end of lexicography, welcome to the machine: On how ChatGPT can already take over all of the dictionary maker's tasks. https://www.youtube.com/watch?v=mEorw0yefAs. 20th CODH Seminar, Center for Open Data in the Humanities, Research Organization of Information and Systems, National Institute of Informatics, Tokyo, Japan.

Vered Shwartz, Enrico Santus, and Dominik Schlechtweg. 2017. Hypernyms under siege: Linguistically-motivated artillery for hypernymy detection. In *Proceedings of the 15th Conference of the European Chapter of the Association for Computational Linguistics: Volume 1, Long Papers*, pages 65–75. Association for Computational Linguistics.

Alberto Simões and José João Almeida. 2008. Bilingual terminology extraction based on translation patterns. *Procesamiento del Lenguaje Natural*, (41):281–288.

Karen Spärck Jones. 1972. A statistical interpretation of term specificity and its application in retrieval. *Journal of Documentation*, 28:11–21.

Frieda Steurs, Ken De Wachter, and Evy De Malsche. 2015. Terminology tools. In Hendrik J. and Kockaert et al., editors, *Handbooks of Linguistics and Communication Science*, pages 222–249. John Benjamins, Amsterdam.

Milan Straka and Jana Straková. 2017. Tokenizing, POS tagging, lemmatizing and parsing UD 2.0 with UDPipe. In *Proceedings of the CoNLL 2017 Shared Task: Multilingual Parsing from Raw Text to Universal Dependencies*, pages 88–99, Vancouver, Canada. Association for Computational Linguistics.

Hanh Thi Hong Tran, Matej Martinc, Jaya Caporusso, Antoine Doucet, and Senja Pollak. 2023. The recent advances in automatic term extraction: A survey.

Fabienne Ville-Ometz, Jean Royauté, and Alain Zasadzinski. 2007. Enhancing in automatic recognition and extraction of term variants with linguistic features. *Terminology. International Journal of Theoretical and Applied Issues in Specialized Communication*, 13(1):35–59.

Lennart Wachowiak, Christian Lang, Barbara Heinisch, and Dagmar Gromann. 2021. Towards Learning Terminological Concept Systems from Multilingual Natural Language Text. In *3rd Conference on Language, Data and Knowledge (LDK 2021)*, volume 93 of *Open Access Series in Informatics (OASIcs)*, pages 22:1–22:18, Dagstuhl, Germany. Schloss Dagstuhl – Leibniz-Zentrum für Informatik.

Julie Weeds and David Weir. 2003. A general framework for distributional similarity. In *Proceedings of the 2003 Conference on Empirical Methods in Natural Language Processing*.

Eugen Wüster. 1979. *Einführung in die allgemeine Terminologielehre und terminologische Lexikographie.* Springer, Wien.

Use of NLP Techniques in Translation by ChatGPT: Case Study

Feyza Dalaylı[1]

Çanakkale Onsekiz Mart University, Türkiye[1]

feyza.dalayli@comu.edu.tr

Abstract

In this research, it is aimed to compare the translations from English to Turkish made by ChatGPT, one of the most advanced artificial intelligences, with the translations made by humans. In this context, an academic 1 page English text was chosen. The text was translated by both ChatGPT and a translator who is an academic in the field of translation and has 10 years of experience. Afterwards, two different translations were examined comparatively by 5 different translators who are experts in their fields. Semi-structured in-depth interviews were conducted with these translators.The aim of this study is to reveal the role of artificial intelligence tools in translation, which are increasing day by day and suggesting that there will be no need for language learning in the future. On the other hand, many translators argue that artificial intelligence and human translations can be understood. Therefore, if artificial intelligence is successful, there will be no profession called translator in the future. This research seems to be very useful in terms of shedding light on the future. The method of this research is semi-structured in-depth interview.

1 Credits

This document is an original research. Feyza Dalaylı conducted and concluded this research alone. No support was received from any person for the continuation of the research. Therefore, as ChatGPT emerged and continued to develop, the researcher realized that it was important to consider the subject in terms of translation. Because the basis of the increase in dialogue in the world is the understanding of individuals belonging to different languages. With ChatGPT, there are many innovations that humanity has achieved thanks to artificial intelligence and technology, which is being talked about more and more day by day. This phenomenon, which was much more difficult in the past, today, thanks to artificial intelligence, individuals can translate any document into any language they want within minutes. The important thing here is not only the translation, but the quality of the translation. To date, many tools continue to translate on the internet. However, ChatGPT's difference is its use of NLP. Thus, the translation is perceived as more natural and as if it was made by human hands. In this context, it was deemed appropriate to conduct a case study in order to better understand the research based on it. For the case study, an NLP-related text in Turkish was translated into English by both ChatGPT and a translator with 10 years of translation experience. Within the scope of the case study, these two translations, together with the original text, were shown to 5 academician translators who are experts in their fields. First of all, they were asked which of the translations was done by artificial intelligence. Thus, the differences between artificial intelligence and human translations were tried to be determined. Semi-structured interviews were conducted with the interviewees. During the literature search, both ChatGPT and NLP studies were scanned. However, when it comes to translation, it has been noticed that the number of studies that discuss ChatGPT and NLP together is low. The reason for this is that ChatGPT started to be used in a relatively recent period.

2 Introduction

In recent years, the rapid advancements in Natural Language Processing (NLP) have sparked transformative changes across various domains, including translation. The integration of NLP techniques into translation processes has garnered significant attention due to its potential to revolutionize the way we bridge linguistic gaps. This article delves into a case study that explores the utilization of NLP techniques in translation, focusing on a comparative evaluation of translations generated by ChatGPT, an AI-powered language model developed by OpenAI, and those crafted by expert human translators. The study investigates the efficacy and intricacies of these translations through the lens of five

Proceedings of the First ConTenNTS Workshop and the 16th BUCC workshop, pages 19–25
Varna, Sep 7, 2023
https://doi.org/10.26615/978-954-452-090-8_003

distinguished academician translators. Through a semi-structured interview methodology, we aim to uncover insights into the strengths, limitations, and nuances associated with NLP-assisted translations.

As NLP technologies continue to evolve, their application in translation has the potential to streamline the process, enhance efficiency, and expand access to multilingual content. However, the challenges posed by idiomatic expressions, cultural nuances, and context preservation remain focal points of concern. This study seeks to contribute to the ongoing discourse surrounding the intersection of NLP and translation by offering a nuanced analysis of translations generated by ChatGPT in comparison to those crafted by human experts. By delving into the perceptions and observations of experienced academic translators, it is intended to shed light on the evolving landscape of translation practices in the era of artificial intelligence driven language models.

The subsequent sections of this article will delve into the methodology employed, the details of the case study, and the insightful findings derived from the semi-structured interviews with the academician translators. Through this exploration, it is intended to provide a comprehensive understanding of the current state, implications and possible future directions of NLP-assisted translation. The integration of NLP techniques into translation processes holds the promise of transforming the translation landscape, yet it also poses important questions about the role of human expertise and the preservation of linguistic and cultural subtleties. This study builds upon this premise by examining the practical implications of NLP-assisted translation through the eyes of those deeply entrenched in the field.

3 NLP and AI

Natural Language Processing (NLP) refers to a field of study within the domain of artificial intelligence (AI) and computational linguistics that focuses on the interaction between computers and human language. NLP seeks to develop computational models and algorithms capable of understanding, analyzing, and generating natural language text and speech (Brown et al., 1990). Natural Language Processing (NLP) is a subfield of Artificial Intelligence (AI) that focuses on enabling computers to understand, interpret, and generate human language. The relationship between NLP and AI is symbiotic, as NLP plays a crucial role in advancing the capabilities of AI systems, while AI techniques contribute to the development of more sophisticated NLP models. At its core, NLP aims to bridge the gap between human language and machine understanding by employing various techniques from linguistics, computer science, and statistics. It involves the application of linguistic and computational theories to process, interpret, and extract meaningful information from unstructured textual data (Bahdanau, Cho and Bengio, 2015).

Researchers and practitioners in NLP employ diverse methodologies, including rule-based approaches, statistical models, machine learning techniques (such as neural networks), and more recently, deep learning architectures. These methodologies enable the development of robust algorithms that can learn from large-scale language data to improve the accuracy and effectiveness of language processing systems (Nilsson, 2010).

NLP has numerous real world applications across various domains, including information retrieval, virtual assistants, chatbots, social media analysis, sentiment monitoring, automated translation services, and healthcare, among others. As the field continues to advance, NLP strives to overcome challenges such as understanding the nuances of human language, handling ambiguity, context sensitivity, and incorporating knowledge from diverse sources to enable machines to effectively communicate and interact with humans in a more natural and intuitive manner.

Over time, NLP has taken place in almost every field of life and continues to take place. Because natural language processing is very successful in conveying many things about human beings. Being able to interact with human-computer, in other words artificial intelligence, with natural language is a significant step. In this way, people's work becomes significantly easier, as artificial intelligence can do what people need to do. On the other hand, when human interaction with artificial intelligence is done with natural language processing, human characteristics can almost be attributed to artificial intelligence. Artificial intelligence performs a large number of operations thanks to natural language processing. Translation is only one of these processes. During translation, when artificial intelligence is based on natural language processing, it has many important separation, combining and distinguishing features.

NLP involves various techniques and methodologies that draw from linguistics, computer science, and machine learning. Various studies have dealt with this issue in great detail. Considering these studies and their results, some important points regarding the relationship between NLP and AI are listed: (Andreev, 1967; Bahdanau, Cho, Bengio, 2015; Berger, Della Pietra, Della Pietra, 1996; Cho, Van Merriënboer, Bahdanau, Bengio, 2014; Collobert, Weston, 2008; Davis, Marcus, 2015;

Foundation of AI: Language is a fundamental aspect of human communication and intelligence. Developing AI systems capable of effectively understanding and generating human language is a significant step toward creating more human-like and capable AI agents.

Language Understanding: NLP techniques help AI systems understand the nuances of human language, including context, semantics, sentiment, and intent. This understanding is crucial for tasks such as chatbots, virtual assistants, sentiment analysis, and information retrieval.

Language Generation: AI systems equipped with NLP capabilities can generate coherent and contextually relevant human-like language. This is used in applications like text generation, content summarization, and language translation.

Machine Translation: AI-powered NLP models have revolutionized machine translation, enabling real-time translation of text between languages. This has far-reaching implications for global communication and collaboration.

Sentiment Analysis: NLP allows AI systems to analyze and interpret the sentiment behind text data, enabling businesses to understand customer opinions, reviews, and feedback on a large scale.

Voice Assistants: Voice-based AI assistants like Siri, Google Assistant, and Alexa heavily rely on NLP to understand spoken language, convert it to text, and execute tasks or provide information based on user queries.

Text Classification: NLP techniques are used for categorizing and classifying text data, which has applications in spam detection, content categorization, and more.

Dialog Systems: AI-driven dialog systems leverage NLP to engage in natural-sounding conversations with users. This is used in customer support, virtual companions, and interactive systems.

Challenges: The relationship between NLP and AI also involves addressing challenges such as ambiguity, context, sarcasm, and cultural variations in language interpretation.

Bu bilgilerden de anlaşıldığı üzere yapay zeka ve NLP teknikleri bir arada kullanıldığında önemli faydalar sağlamaktadır. Bütün bunlar

4 NLP, Translation and AI

Natural Language Processing (NLP) and translation are interconnected fields that share a symbiotic relationship, as NLP techniques and methodologies greatly contribute to the advancement and effectiveness of machine translation systems. NLP, a subfield of artificial intelligence (AI), focuses on the interaction between computers and human language. It encompasses a wide range of tasks, including text analysis, syntactic and semantic parsing, sentiment analysis, information extraction, and machine translation (Bahdanau, Cho and Bengio, 2014).

NMT models employ deep learning architectures, such as recurrent neural networks (RNNs) and more specifically, long short term memory (LSTM) networks, to learn the mapping between source and target language sentences. These models are trained on large scale parallel corpora, consisting of aligned sentence pairs in different languages. The training process involves optimizing model parameters to minimize the discrepancy between predicted translations and human-generated translations (Wu et al., 2016)

NLP techniques are crucial at various stages of machine translation. Preprocessing techniques, such as tokenization, sentence segmentation, and morphological analysis, help break down input text into meaningful linguistic units, making it easier for translation models to process and understand the content. Syntactic and semantic parsing techniques aid in capturing the structural and semantic relationships within sentences, improving the overall coherence and accuracy of translations. Furthermore, NLP-based methods are employed for handling specific translation challenges, such as handling idiomatic expressions, resolving lexical ambiguities, and addressing syntactic divergences between languages. For instance, statistical alignment models, based on NLP algorithms, enable the identification of correspondences between words or phrases in source and target languages, facilitating the generation of more accurate translations. Several studies have demonstrated the effectiveness of NLP techniques in enhancing machine translation quality. For example, Bahdanau et al. (2015) introduced the attention mechanism, an NLP technique that enables NMT models to focus on relevant parts of the source sentence during translation. This attention mechanism significantly improved the translation quality of neural machine translation models.

5 ChatGPT, NLP and Translation

ChatGPT is a language model developed by OpenAI that utilizes the principles of Natural Language Processing (NLP) for various tasks, including translations. NLP is a field of artificial intelligence that focuses on the interaction between computers and human language. It encompasses a range of techniques and algorithms for processing, analyzing, and understanding natural language. When it comes to translation, NLP techniques can be applied to facilitate the conversion of text from one language to another. ChatGPT employs a sequence-to-sequence model, a type of neural network architecture commonly used in machine translation tasks. This model takes an input sequence in one language and generates a corresponding output sequence in the target language (OpenAI, 2023).

The training process for ChatGPT involves exposing the model to large amounts of multilingual data, allowing it to learn patterns, syntax, and semantic relationships across different languages. This exposure enables the model to develop a general understanding of language structures and meanings, making it capable of performing translation tasks. To enhance translation quality, ChatGPT leverages the Transformer architecture, which has been highly successful in NLP tasks. Transformers utilize attention mechanisms, enabling the model to focus on different parts of the input sequence during the translation process. This attention mechanism allows the model to capture long-range dependencies and improve the overall coherence and accuracy of translations. Additionally, techniques such as subword tokenization, which divides words into smaller units, are commonly employed in NLP translation systems like ChatGPT. Subword tokenization helps handle out-of-vocabulary words and improves the model's ability to handle rare or unknown words (GPT-4 Technical Report, 2023).

As can be seen, there have been significant developments in artificial intelligence translations thanks to NLP. However, it is not possible to say that it has fully reached the quality of translation made by people. The only goal in artificial intelligence translations is to reach translations made by humans. In general, there are some fundamental differences between human and ChatGPT translations.

Human-made translations and translations generated by ChatGPT (or similar language models) have several key differences (Kelly and Zetzsche, 2014; Koehn, 2010; Sutskever, Vinyals and Le, 2014; Costa-jussà and Fonollosa, 2016)

Translation Quality: Human translators are capable of producing high-quality translations with a deep understanding of both the source and target languages. They can accurately capture the nuances, cultural references, idioms, and context of the original text. On the other hand, ChatGPT translations can sometimes be less accurate or may not fully grasp the intended meaning due to the limitations of the training data and the model's inability to comprehend context in the same way a human can. While ChatGPT can provide reasonable translations, they may lack the finesse and precision of a human translator.

Natural Language Processing: Human translators are skilled at processing and understanding natural language, taking into account the broader context, cultural implications, and the intended audience. They can adapt their translations to suit the target audience, tone, and purpose of the text. ChatGPT, although trained on a vast amount of text data, lacks the same level of natural language understanding. It often relies on pattern matching and statistical analysis to generate translations, which can result in less nuanced or contextually appropriate outputs.

Subject Matter Expertise: Human translators often specialize in specific domains or subject areas, allowing them to have deep knowledge and understanding of technical or specialized terminology. They can accurately translate complex or industry-specific texts, ensuring the meaning is preserved. ChatGPT, while having access to a wide range of general knowledge, may struggle with domain-specific vocabulary or terminology, leading to inaccuracies or incorrect translations in specialized texts.

Cultural Sensitivity: Human translators are well-versed in the cultural nuances of both the source and target languages. They can navigate potential pitfalls, adapt the translation to the cultural context, and avoid unintended offensive or inappropriate language choices. ChatGPT lacks this level of cultural sensitivity and may produce translations that are culturally tone-deaf or insensitive, as it lacks the ability to understand the subtleties and implications of language choices.

Revision and Editing: Human translators go through an iterative process of revision and editing to refine their translations, ensuring accuracy, clarity, and quality. They can self-correct errors and refine their translations based on feedback or additional research. ChatGPT, while capable of generating translations, does not have the same ability to self-correct or improve based on feedback. It generates translations in a single pass, without the iterative refinement process that humans can employ.

In summary, while ChatGPT can be a useful tool for generating translations, human-made translations generally outperform machine-generated translations in terms of quality, accuracy, contextuality, cultural sensitivity, and domain-specific expertise.

In conclusion, NLP and machine translation are closely intertwined, with NLP providing essential tools, methodologies, and techniques that contribute to the development and improvement of machine translation systems. The integration of NLP methods has led to significant advancements in translation accuracy, fluency, and the ability to handle various linguistic complexities. As NLP continues to evolve, its impact on the field of machine translation is expected to grow, enabling the creation of more sophisticated and context-aware translation systems.

6 Method

The in-depth interview method is a qualitative research technique used to gather detailed and comprehensive data from participants by engaging them in a structured conversation. This method allows researchers to explore complex phenomena, understand individuals' perspectives, and obtain rich insights into their experiences. In-depth interview method was also used in this study. In this context, a text was chosen first. This text has been translated by both ChatGPT and a lecturer who is a professor in the field of foreign language and translation science. Then, these two translation sources were ambiguously shown to 5 expert academician translators and in-depth interviews were conducted on translations.

7 Findings

The findings of the study are quite remarkable. First of all, 3 of 5 academician translators thought that a translator translated the text translated with ChatGPT and stated that the translation was of high quality. On the other hand, the remaining 2 interviewees insisted that both translations were of good quality, even if they were aware of the translation made with ChatGPT. All interviewees stated that the reason why ChatGPT, which translates via artificial intelligence, is so good is that it uses NLP techniques correctly and appropriately. An interviewer who noticed the translation made only with ChatGPT, stated that a few sentences were robotic and cold, and thus he thought that the translation was not translated by humans. As it can be understood from here, although ChatGPT has made significant progress in translation, it has not been able to prevent some of its expressions from being cold and far from human sincerity. This shows that it still needs to make progress on NLP. In addition to all these, it is an important detail that only 1 of 5 academician translators who have been working in the sector and academic field for more than 10 years noticed this detail.

The interviewees also evaluated the future of the relationship between ChatGPT and NLP. Accordingly, there is a possibility that the translators' jobs will become much easier in the future, and there may even be times when translators are no longer needed. The interviewees underlined that certain criteria should be taken into account when it comes to translation. Accordingly, a translation should include a wide variety of components such as grammar rules, correct and appropriate use of expressions, naturalness, fluidity, and the general structure of the translated language. In response to these statements, the interviewees were asked to evaluate the differences between ChatGPT's current status and artificial intelligence translations in the past. It was confirmed by all interviewees that the development in NLP practices was the basis of these developments.

The interviewees were asked to express the differences between the two translations. The main purpose here is to identify the main differences between artificial intelligence and human translations. Interestingly, 3 interviewees who thought that artificial intelligence translation was human translation first suggested that the translation was natural and sufficient in terms of terminology. From this point of view, the level of development of ChatGPT in terms of human spontaneity and adequate terminology can be seen.

On the other hand, while it is an important finding that the translations made with ChatGPT are not noticed in general, the interviewees also put forward the quality and smoothness of the translation as a reason. As it can be understood from here, ChatGPT has managed to increase the quality of translation in this sense, as it receives NLP support. Although the interviewees are translators, they support the development of artificial intelligence in the future and replacing people when necessary in translation.

Finally, the interviewees were asked to evaluate the use of NLP in artificial intelligence supported tools within the scope of translation. Except for 1 interviewee, all interviewees stated that these tools will play a positive role in the development of intercultural communication by bringing humanity to an important point in translation and foreign language development in the future. However, one interviewee stated that the development of these tools harmed humanity rather than contributed. According to him, foreign language learning will decrease among people in the future as these tools make people lazy. Thanks to instant translation, people will only communicate with the help of tools without learning anything new. This will cause humanity to move away from naturalness day by day and become robotic. Although one interviewee expressed her fears about the future with these statements, the development of ChatGPT in translation is generally appreciated by the interviewees.

8 Conclusion

Undoubtedly, the most important area where natural language processing is visible to the translator is machine translation. When the development of translation from the time it first emerged to the present, it cannot be ignored that a very important point has been reached today. In particular, the development of artificial intelligence tools such as ChatGPT is considered a turning point in translation. ChatGPT is capable of rendering quality translations that are almost indistinguishable from human translations today. Although it still needs improvement, ChatGPT has made significant improvements in translation. The basis of these developments and improvements is the correct and appropriate use of NLP techniques. Considering that artificial intelligence tools such as ChatGPT will increase in the future, the deficiencies that exist today will be eliminated with the NLP systems that will develop. Although there were hopeless and frightening opinions about the future among the interviewees, in general, this case study shows that NLP-supported artificial intelligence applications are beneficial for humanity. The translation done by ChatGPT was perceived by most of the interviewees as being done by a human translator. This clearly demonstrates progress. Thanks to artificial intelligence NLP, it has made a remarkable improvement in translation based on the way people think and express. As long as ChatGPT continues to receive support from NLP, it will be much more successful in the future.

According to the general results of the research, NLP enabled the positive development of artificial intelligence supported translation tools. Thus, artificial intelligence, which can replace human beings in the field of translation and alleviate the workload, will become even more important in the near future. This is supported by most of the translators. The perception of translations made by artificial intelligence such as ChatGPT as if they are made by humans is associated with translation quality, naturalness, subject-verb harmony and general harmony in sentences.

Bibliography

Andreev N.D. 1967. *The intermediary language as the focal point of machine translation. In: Booth AD (ed) Machine translation.* North Holland Publishing Company, Amsterdam

Bahdanau, D., Cho, K. and Bengio Y. 2015. *Neural machine translation by jointly learning to align and translate*. In International Conference on Learning Representation. https://arxiv.org/pdf/1409.0473.pdf.

Berger A.L, Della Pietra S.A, Della Pietra V.J. 1996. *A maximum entropy approach to natural language processing*. Computational Linguistics 22(1), 39-71

Brown, P. F., Cocke, J., Pietra, S. A. D., Pietra, V. J. D., Jelinek, F., Lafferty, J. D., Mercer, R. L., and Roossin, P. S. A. 1990. *Statistical approach to machine translation*. Compu-tational linguistics. 16(2), 79–85.

Cho K, Van Merriënboer B, Bahdanau D, Bengio Y. 2014. *On the properties of neural machine translation: encoder-decoder approaches*. https://arxiv.org/pdf/1409.1259.pdf.

Collobert R. Weston J. 2008. *A unified architecture for natural language processing*. In proceedings of the 25th international conference on machine learning (pp. 160–167)

Costa-jussà M.R.and Fonollosa, J.A.R. 2016. Character-based Neural Machine Translation, Proc. of the ACL, pp, 357-361.

Davis E., Marcus G. 2015. *Commonsense reasoning and commonsense knowledge in artificial intelligence*. Commun ACM 58(9), 92–103.

GPT-4 Technical Report, https://arxiv.org/abs/2303.08774, last accessed 2023/06/16.

Kelly, N., Zetzsche, J. 2014. *Found in Translation: How Language Shapes Our Lives and Transforms the World*. 1st edn. Penguin Book, USA.

Koehn, P. 2010. *Statistical Machine Translation*. 2nd edn, Cambridge University Press, UK.

Nilsson, N. J. 2010. *The Quest For AI- A History of Ideas and Achievements*. http://ai.standford.edu/~nilsson/.

OpenAI, https://openai.com/blog/chatgpt/, last accessed 2023/06/20.

Sutskever, I., Vinyals, O., & Le, Q. V. 2014. *Sequence to Sequence Learning with Neural Networks. Advances in Neural Information Processing Systems*. 1-9. https://arxiv.org/pdf/1409.3215.pdf.

Wu,Y. Schuster, M., Chen, Z., Le, Q. V. and Norouzi M. 2016. *Google's Neural Machine Translation System: Bridging the Gap between Human and Machine Translation*. https://arxiv.org/pdf/1609.08144.pdf.

On the Evaluation of Terminology Translation Errors in NMT and PB-SMT In the Legal Domain: A Study on the Translation of Arabic Legal Documents into English and French

Khadija Ait ElFqih[1] and Johanna Monti[1]

[1]UNIOR NLP Research Group, University of Naples 'L'Orientale'
{kaitelfqih, jmonti@unior.it}

Abstract

In the translation process, terminological resources are used to solve translation problems, so information on terminological equivalence is crucial to make the most appropriate choices in terms of translation equivalence. In the context of Machine translation, indeed, neural models have improved the state-of-the-art in Machine Translation considerably in recent years. However, they still underperform in domain-specific fields and in under-resourced languages. This is particularly evident in translating legal terminology for Arabic, where current Machine Translation outputs do not adhere to the contextual, linguistic, cultural, and terminological constraints posed by translating legal terms in Arabic. In this paper, we conduct a comparative qualitative evaluation and comprehensive error analysis on legal terminology translation in Phrase-Based Statistical Machine Translation and Neural Machine Translation in two language pairs: Arabic-English, Arabic-French. We propose an error typology taking the legal terminology translation from Arabic into account. We demonstrate our findings highlighting the strengths and weaknesses of both approaches in the area of legal terminology translation for Arabic. We also introduce a multilingual gold standard dataset that we developed using our Arabic legal corpus. This dataset serves as a reliable benchmark and/or reference during the evaluation process to decide the degree of adequacy and fluency of the Phrase-Based Statistical Machine Translation and Neural Machine Translation systems.

1 Introduction

Machine Translation (MT) is a subfield of computational linguistics that draws its fundamentals from linguistics, computer science, information theory, artificial intelligence, and statistics (Sepesy Maučec & Donaj, 2019). Phrase-Based Statistical Machine Translation (PB-SMT) (Koehn et al., 2003), a predictive modelling approach to MT, was the main paradigm in MT research for more than two decades. Neural Machine Translation (NMT) (Kalchbrenner et al., 2014; Cho et al., 2014; Nishimura & Akiba, 2017; Vaswani et al., 2017), the current paradigm for MT research, is an approach to automatic translation in which a large neural network is trained by deep learning techniques. Over the last five years, there has been incremental progress in the field of NMT (Koehn, 2020; Herold et al., 2022; Almahasees, 2021; Rossi & Carre, 2022) to the point where some researchers claim parity with human translation (Thierry, 2022). Consistent term translation is an important facet of quality assurance for specialized translation. Since terminologies are essential for communication among domain experts, term forms must be consistent and their translation must respond to the contextual requirements to maintain the integrity of the underlying conceptual system during knowledge exchange (Darwish, 2009; Sager, 1990). Nevertheless, some knowledge domains and languages still suffer from the lack of high-quality MT results due to the mistranslation of terminology (Mediouni, 2016; Killman, 2014; Zakraoui et al., 2021). This is the case, especially in the legal domain and the Arabic language. Consider example 1 from the Moroccan family code, taking the terms 'الفراش', 'الطعن', 'اللعان', 'القطع' into consideration:

Proceedings of the First ConTenNTS Workshop and the 16th BUCC workshop, pages 26–35
Varna, Sep 7, 2023
https://doi.org/10.26615/978-954-452-090-8_004

1. **AR:** يعتبر **الفراش** بشروطه حجة قاطعة على ثبوت النسب, لا يمكن **الطعن** فيه إلا من الزوج عن طريق **اللعان**, أو بواسطة خبرة تفيد **القطع**.

   EN (NMT): The **Mattress**, with its conditions, is considered a definitive proof of Paternity, and it can only be **challenged** by the husband through **li'an**, or by means of experience that proves the **severance**.

   EN (HT): The **Marriage consummation** is considered a strong proof of paternity; it can be **rebutted** only by the husband through **accusation** or **certain** evidence.

   FR (PB-SMT): La **literie** selon ses termes est un argument concluant pour établir la filiation, qui ne peut être **contestée** par le mari que par la **baise**, ou par l'expérience de la coupe, par deux conditions : le mari en question apporte une preuve solide de sa demande; Un mandat a été émis pour cette expertise.

   FR (HT): La **consommation du mariage** est considérée comme une preuve solide signifiant la paternité, il ne peut être **réfutée** que par le mari soit à travers **l'accusation** ou bien une **certaine** preuve.

The bold terms in example 1 are domain-specific and context-dependent, so their correct translation requires the consideration of the context, as well as of the cultural, lexical, morphological, and semantic properties of the terms in addition to their equivalences across languages and legal systems (i.e., English, and French), as the HT does. Both NMT and PB-SMT, instead, produce wrong results. This example highlights the main weaknesses of MT, namely lack of terminology resources related to the legal domain for Arabic, the lack of training on Arabic legal texts to render the appropriate equivalences, and the terminology linguistic characteristics of this type of discourse.

In this work, we aim to compare PB-SMT and NMT with reference to terminology translation by carrying out an extensively detailed manual evaluation. We propose an error typology taking the legal terminology translation from Arabic into account. While automatic metrics provide a quick and cost-effective way to evaluate MT output (Zakraoui et al., 2021; Sepesy Maučec & Donaj, 2020), it is not recommended for evaluating terminology translation errors (Izwaini, 2006; Gamal et al., 2022; Haque et al., 2020; Killman, 2014) because they have limitations in assessing the accuracy, quality, legal context, and cultural nuances of legal translations for Arabic. For this reason, we create a multilingual gold standard dataset (AR-EN / AR-FR) using a corpus of judicial documents (i.e., contracts, provisions, codes, decrees) of different Arab countries (Morocco, Algeria, Tunisia, United Arab Emirates, Saudi Arabia, Egypt) specifically created for this experiment. This multilingual dataset is used as a benchmark for evaluating both the NMT and PB-SMT results concerning out-of-context and in-context legal terms. To ensure the quality and reliability of the reference translations of the gold standard dataset, we collaborate with a legal expert and an Arab linguist who are proficient in both the source and target languages.

2 Related Work

Since the introduction of NMT to the MT community, researchers have been analyzing the pros and cons of NMT compared to PB-SMT. Koehn & Knowles (2017) examine several challenges to NMT and give empirical results on how well the technology holds up compared to PB-SMT. To do this, they train both NMT and PB-SMT for German-English on domains that are quite distant from each other (i.e., law (Acquis), Medical (EMEA), IT, Koran (Tanzil), subtitles) obtained from OPUS (Tiedemann, 2012). They note that the output of the NMT system is often quite fluent but completely unrelated to the input, while the PB-SMT output betrays its difficulties with coping with the out-of-domain input by leaving some words untranslated. They conclude that despite the recent successes, NMT must still overcome various challenges, most notably performance in out-of-domain and under-resourced conditions. Zakraoui et al. (2021) conduct a survey related to Arabic MT challenges which they split into two categories, namely linguistic (i.e., morphology richness, syntactic word reordering, Word Sense Disambiguation, vocalization, dialectal variation, gender bias, etc.) and technical (i.e., low-resource language, domain mismatch, Out-Of-Vocabulary, word alignment, sentence length, among others). Several studies including Alsohybe et al (2017); Hadla et al (2014); Han (2016) prove the ineffectiveness of NMT systems, mainly Google Translate (GT) when producing Arabic-English translations. In the context of domain-specific translation, particularly when dealing with legal texts, the problem escalates significantly. This is mainly due to domain mismatch (Koehn, 2020), which Wang et al., (2020) tackle using multi-domain NMT.

As long as the MT evaluation is concerned, researchers use different metrics such as Word Error Rate (Sai et al., 2022), METEOR (Lavie & Denkowski, 2009; Banerjee & Lavie, 2005), AL-BLEU (Bouamor et al., 2014) metric which extends BLEU (Papineni et al., 2002) to deal with Arabic rich morphology. Nevertheless, Han, (2016) and another recent study by Lee et al., (2023) try to evaluate several automatic metrics, including the above ones. They prove that no conclusions can be drawn on the superior performance of any specific metric over others. They state that while automatic metrics such as BLEU, capture the average case for how well an MT model translates sentences, they do not give insights into which linguistic aspects MT models struggle with producing fluent output. In this regard, some efforts investigate statistical error analysis of MT for Arabic with native speakers so they can review linguistic aspects of MT errors (El Marouani et al., 2020; Al Mahasees 2020), while others use neural networks to detect errors (Madi & Al-Khalifa, 2020) for Arabic texts or to correct them (Watson et al., 2018). In another study on evaluating terminology translation in MT, Haque et al., (2019) examine why the automatic evaluation techniques fail to distinguish term translation in few cases, and identify the reasons (e.g., reordering, and inflectional issues in term translation). In this regard, they propose the TermEval metric for the automatic evaluation of terminology translation in MT. Nevertheless, the proposed metric supports only the English-Hindi pair because of resources limitation.

We now turn our attention to studies related to terminology translation in MT. Haque et al. (2020) investigate legal domain term translation in PB-SMT and NMT with two morphologically divergent languages, English and Hindi. In their experiment, they adopt a technique that semi-automatically creates a gold standard test set from an English-Hindi judicial domain parallel corpus. The sentences of the gold standard test set are translated with their PB-SMT and NMT systems, and the patterns of the terminology translation errors on a sample set of translations is inspected and classified. A comparative evaluation of PB-SMT and NMT on terminology translation is then carried out. They find that NMT is less prone to errors than PB-SMT as far as terminology translation is concerned (8.3% versus 9.9% and 11.5% versus 12.9% error rates in English-Hindi and Hindi-English translation tasks, respectively; differences in error rates are statistically significant). Their empirical results present divergent outcomes in comparison to those reported in several prior investigations (Vintar, 2018; Dugonik et al. 2023; Khazin et al. 2023). In another scenario, Müller et al. (2019) study the performance of PB-SMT and NMT systems on out-of-domain German-English OPUS data and German-Romansh to define five domains (i.e., medical, IT, koran, law, and subtitles). They find that in unknown domains, PB-SMT and NMT suffer from different problems: PB-SMT systems are mostly adequate but not fluent, while NMT systems are mostly fluent but not adequate. For NMT, they identify hallucinations (translations that are fluent but unrelated to the source) as a key reason for low domain robustness. Several studies, including Al-Shehab (2013); Killman (2014); Junczys-Dowmunt et al. (2016); Baruah & Singh (2023), prove that although NMT systems are known to generalize better than phrase-based systems for out-of-domain data, it is unclear how they perform in purely in-domain setting, especially in the legal domain from Arabic where terminology translation remains questionable and subject to continuous post-edition (Alkatheery, 2023). Given all the serious translation issues that Arabic terminology in the legal domain faces, it remains a poorly explored area in MT research. Hence, extensive research efforts are still needed to enhance and refine these aspects.

3 Experiments Set-up and Methodology

To conduct our study, we semi-automatically create a gold standard dataset[1] from our legal corpus that we created using a variety of legal documents (i.e., codes, contracts, provisions, constitutions, and decrees) of different Arab countries. The resource setup is described in detail in Table 3 and in ElFqih et al. (2023), and, to the best of our knowledge, this is the first formalized resource created specifically for assessing the

[1]Available here: https://github.com/Kaitelfqih/Gold-standard-Terminology-Translation-Evaluation-Data-Set

accuracy and adequacy of MT outputs regarding terminology in the legal domain for Arabic against English and French. This terminology resource consists of:

- 1015 out-of-context legal term translated using NMT system (GT) and PB-SMT system (RC),
- 1015 in-context legal term translated using NMT system (GT) and PB-SMT system (RC),
- Manual annotations of NMT and PB-SMT errors (see section 4),
- 1015 Reference translations for both out-of-context and in-context dataset validated by a legal expert.

To address our research objectives, our methodology unfolds four distinct phases, to investigate key aspects of the study. They are as follow:

- The translation of the out-of-context and in-context terms from Arabic to English, and French using GT and RC,
- The extraction of phrases using NooJ grammars[2] (Silberztein, 2015) containing the terms list understudy,
- The production of the reference translations of the legal terms for Arabic according to online gateways of EU laws, including EUR-Lex[3], IATE[4], Juremy[5],

Our reference translations undergo thorough annotation and validation processes conducted by two skilled annotators:

- The first annotator is a legal expert whose language skills are excellent both in the source and the target languages. He validates the translations after checking their degree of accuracy and adequacy in the target languages.
- The second annotator, a native Arabic speaker with a linguistic background meticulously annotates the Part-of-Speech tags, Geographical Usage (following the ISO 20771:2020 standard for Legal translation Requirements, to indicate where a given term is adapted to express a legal practice).

The above steps are important for the sake of placing equivalence references which ensure an adequate and accurate analysis. The annotators possess a deep understanding of legal concepts and the nuances of the Arabic language. Their combined expertise ensures the accuracy and reliability of the annotations present in the dataset. This dual-annotator approach enhances the quality of the data by reducing the chances of errors and inconsistencies, and it provides a standardized point of reference for evaluating PB-SMT and NMT systems objectively and systematically in the area of legal terminology translation for Arabic.

The second phase of the experiment focuses on manual evaluation carried out by a native Arabic speaker. It consists of a systematic analysis where we classify and annotate the errors (see Section 4) of machine-translated out-of-context and in-context legal terms from AR to EN and FR produced by different MT systems (GT and RC). Figure 1 displays the number of terms and sentences containing errors, along with their corresponding percentages in Table 1 and Table 2.

Table 1: Error Types of Machine-Translated Out-of-Context Legal Terms for Arabic.

	Arabic-English		Arabic-French	
Errors	NMT	PB-SMT	NMT	PB-SMT
Ambiguity Errors (AE)				
Cultural and Legal Systems Relatedness Errors (CLSRE)	63%	62%	58%	56%
Register Errors (RE)				
Transliteration Errors (TE)				
Gender Bias Errors (GBE)	35%	33%	38%	40%
None of the Above (Ø)	2%	5%	4%	4%

[2]https://nooj.univ-fcomte.fr/

[3]https://eur-lex.europa.eu/browse/eurovoc.html?locale=en

[4]https://iate.europa.eu/home

[5]https://www.juremy.com/

Table 2 : Error Types of Machine-Translated In-Context Legal Terms for Arabic

	Arabic-English		Arabic-French	
Errors	**NMT**	**PB-SMT**	**NMT**	**PB-SMT**
Reordering Errors (RE)				
Ambiguity Errors (AE)				
Cultural and Legal Systems Relatedness Errors (CLSRE)	65.2%	63.8%	63.5%	65.5%
Register Errors (RE)				
Transliteration Errors (TE)				
Lexical Repetition Errors (LRE)	32.8%	31.2%	31.5%	32.5%
Term Drop Errors (TDR)				
Gender Bias Errors (GBE)				
None of the Above (Ø)	2%	5%	5%	2%

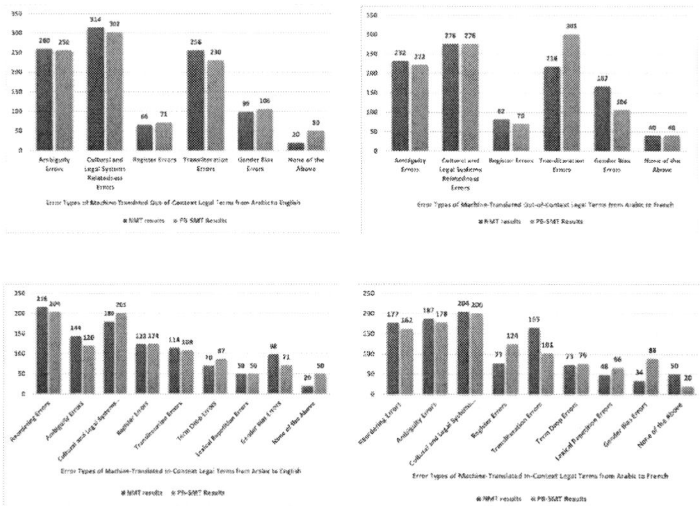

Figure 1: Graphs Showing the Detailed Numbers of Out-of-Context (Upper Graph) and In-Context (Lower Graph) Terms and Their Respective Errors in NMT and PB-SMT Systems from Arabic into English and French

4 Evaluation and Results

The errors posed by machine-translated legal terms for Arabic are classified into six error types for out-of-context terms (Table 1) and in eight types for in-context terms (Table 2).

Table 1 and Table 2 show the manual evaluation results after comparing the outputs of NMT and PB-SMT systems from AR to EN and FR against the gold test-set. Figure 1 provides a detailed overview of the number of both the Out-of-Context and in In-Context legal terms along with the errors identified through the manual evaluation for each context.

Table 1 presents the results of the evaluation of the correspondence between NMT and PB-SMT systems of out-of-context legal terms in AR-EN/AR-FR pairs, indicating the number of terms that contain the errors and their respective percentage.

For AR-EN, NMT appears to be more error-prone than PB-SMT. NMT commits 36% of errors related to AE, CLSRE, RE, and below 40% of errors related to TE and GBE. Whereas PB-SMT presents 62% of errors related to AE, CLSRE, RE, and below 33% of errors related to TE and GBE. In addition, only 2% in NMT and 5% in PB-SMT are correct translations. For the AR-FR pair, NMT preserves its status of being more erroneous than PB-SMT, where NMT presents a percentage of 58% of errors related to AE, CLSRE, RE, and 38% in favor of TE and GBE. Whereas PB-SMT achieves 56% of AE, CLSRE, RE, but outperforms NMT with 40% of errors related to TE and GBE.

In addition, 4% in NMT and 4% in PB-SMT are correct translations.

Table 2 includes the manual evaluation results of in-context machine-translated legal sentences where the terms in Table 1 are spotted. The findings for NMT and PB-SMT for AR-EN/ AR-FR show that the percentage and number of errors obtained after translating the terms in context increase in comparison with the previous results (Table 1) obtained for out-of-context terms. In other words, for AR-EN pairs, NMT seems to exhibit a higher percentage of errors compared to PB-SMT, and vice versa for AR-FR pairs. However, the incidence rate is higher in errors related to RE, AE, CLSRE, RE. The findings reveal that the inclusion of contextual information makes it hard for the MT systems to mitigate these errors and produce accurate legal translations for Arabic, consider example 1:

1. **AR:** **حكم** القاضي بتاريخ 2011/01/01 بجميع ما للزوجة على الزوج من **واجبات** من **نفقة** و **متعة**.
   EN (NMT): The judge **ruled** on 01/01/2011 all the **duties** of the wife to the husband of **maintenance** and **pleasure**.
   EN (HT): On 01/01/2011, the judge **sentenced** that the husband must comply with all the wife's **rights**, including **expenditure** and **compensation**.
   FR (SMT): Le juge a **statué** le 01/01/2011 sur l'ensemble des **devoirs** de la femme envers le mari **d'entretien** et de **jouissance**.
   FR (HT): Le 01/01/2011, le juge a **condamné** le mari à respecter tous les **droits** de sa femme, y compris les **dépenses** et **l'indemnisation**.

The bold terms in example 1 are domain-specific and context-dependent these factors make their accurate translation a complex process. The HT, indeed, considers various elements, including context, exact terminology choice, structure, syntax, as well as their compatibility across languages and legal systems. Whereas NMT and PB-SMT systems fail in producing quality translations due to errors, such as:

- RE, which disrupts the sentence structure, leading to confusion in the intended meaning of legal terms, and which might not align with the conventions of legal writing in Arabic, potentially affecting the legal validity and clarity of the text,
- AE that creates multiple interpretations of legal terms, causing uncertainty and potential misinterpretations in legal documents,
- CLSRE where certain concepts or practices does not exist in the target legal system, leading to inappropriate or misleading translations because legal texts and terms are deeply influenced by the cultural and historical context of the legal system they belong to,
- TDE where MT systems omit the source term in translation,
- LRE when translation of a source term, is an incorrect lexical choice,
- GBE which significantly impacts legal translation from Arabic into English and French, as these languages have different ways of handling gender in their grammatical structures and legal systems.

Our corpus consists of judicial documents (i.e., contracts, provisions, codes, decrees) of different Arab countries (Morocco, Algeria, Tunisia, United Arab Emirates, Saudi Arabia, Egypt). Therefore, the use of distinct legal terminology to convey similar legal practices in different countries can significantly impact the outcomes of MT for Arabic. Due to variations in legal systems, cultural nuances, idiomatic expressions, linguistic variations, and the specific precision required in legal language, MT may struggle to accurately capture the intended meanings. This could lead to mistranslations, misinterpretations, and errors that have potentially serious legal consequences. For example, the term **'مأذون'** is used mostly in Qatar and Egypt. It is used to refer to the person certified by the judge to perform certain legal formalities, especially to draw up or certify marriage contracts, deeds, and other documents for use in other jurisdictions [6]. RC, however, translates it as **'authorized'** into English and **'autorisé'** into French. Whereas GT, as well, translates it as **'authorized'** into English and **'autorisé'** into French. Therefore, we notice that both systems not only transform the grammatical category of the term from a noun, which represents a person into an adjective, but they also misinterpret the intended

[6]https://www.almaany.com/ar/dict/ar-ar/

legal practice in the target legal systems. Hence, in France, the equivalence of 'مأذون' is **'maire'** (i.e., the person who chairs the municipal council[7]), he/she is the one who oversees approving and drawing up marriage contracts. Whereas in England the person in charge of approving and celebrating the marriage requests is called the **'superintendent registrar[8]'** of the district.

This unveils that MT systems are not trained on a diverse and comprehensive dataset that covers a wide range of legal terminologies from different countries. In other words, MT systems need to be equipped with region-specific legal dictionaries and context-aware algorithms that consider the nuances of each country's legal language. Additionally, leveraging parallel legal texts in different terms can help train MT models to better handle these variations.

5 Conclusion and Future Work

In this paper, we conduct a comparative qualitative evaluation and comprehensive error analysis on legal terminology translation between PB-SMT and NMT in two translation pairs: AR-EN/ AR-FR. We also introduce a multilingual gold standard dataset that we developed using our Arabic legal corpus, which serves as a reliable benchmark and/or reference during the evaluation process to decide the degree of adequacy and fluency of the PB-SMT and NMT systems. We propose an error typology taking the legal terminology translation from Arabic into account.

We demonstrate our findings, highlighting the strengths and weaknesses of both approaches to MT in legal terminology translation for Arabic. We found that NMT is more error-prone than PB-SMT in both language pairs when translating out-of-context terms. Whereas, for the AR-EN pair, NMT seems to exhibit a higher percentage of errors compared to PB-SMT concerning in-context machine-translated legal terms. Concerning the AR-FR language pair, although NMT and PB-SMT have the same overall error rate (94%) NMT produces more errors related to RE, AE, CLSRE, and register errors.

The findings also demonstrate that despite advances in MT, legal translation remains a challenging task that demands precision and adherence to specific legal nuances. For critical legal documents, human translation by professional legal experts is still the preferred approach to ensure the highest level of accuracy and consistency. MT, however, can be a helpful tool for initial draft translations or to aid human translators, but it should be used with caution, especially for legal content.

As future work, a second annotator will undertake the annotation of the data concerning the MT errors, and the assessment of inter-annotator agreement will be conducted to enhance the reliability of the data.

We will afterward focus on developing a high-quality multilingual corpus from AR-EN/ AR-FR in the legal domain to enhance the performance of MT systems. Careful attention will be given to aligning sentences with precise legal terminologies to provide reliable and contextual translations.

References

AlMahasees, Z. (2020). Diachronic evaluation of Google Translate, Microsoft Translator, and Sakhr in English-Arabic translation [Master thesis]. Unpublished Master's Thesis, the University of Western Australia, Australia.

Alkatheery, E. R. (2023). Google translate errors in legal texts: Machine translation quality assessment. Center for Open Science. http://dx.doi.org/10.31235/osf.io/j4zh7

Al-Rukban, A., & Saudagar, A. K. J. (2017, December 20). Evaluation of English to Arabic Machine Translation Systems using BLEU and GTM. Proceedings of the 2017 9th International Conference on Education Technology and Computers. http://dx.doi.org/10.1145/3175536.3175570

Al-Shehab, M. (2013). The translatability of English legal sentences into Arabic by using Google translation. International Journal of English Language and Linguistics Research, 1(3), 18–31.

Alsohybe, N., Dahan, N., & BaAlwi, F. (2017). Machine-Translation history and evolution: Survey for Arabic-english translations. Current Journal of Applied Science and Technology, 23(4), 1–19. https://doi.org/10.9734/cjast/2017/36124

Banerjee, S., & Lavie, A. (2005). METEOR: An automatic metric for MT evaluation with improved

[7]EESC/COR-FR, d'après le Conseil des communes et régions d'Europe (CCRE), «Gouvernements locaux et régionaux en Europe — Structures et compétences» (2016) (3.5.2022), page 26

[8]Term reference: https://www.citizensadvice.org.uk/family/living-together-marriage-and-civil-partnership/getting-married/

correlation with human judgments. Proceedings of the Acl Workshop on Intrinsic and Extrinsic Evaluation Measures for Machine Translation and/or Summarization, 65–72.

Baruah, R., & Singh, A. K. (2023). A clinical practice by machine translation on low resource languages. In Natural Language Processing in Healthcare (pp. 1–17). CRC Press. http://dx.doi.org/10.1201/9781003138013-1

Berrichi, S., & Mazroui, A. (2021). Addressing limited vocabulary and long sentences constraints in english–arabic neural machine translation. Arabian Journal for Science and Engineering, 46(9), 8245–8259. https://doi.org/10.1007/s13369-020-05328-2

Bouamor, H., Alshikhabobakr, H., Mohit, B., & Of lazer, K. (2014). A human judgement corpus and a metric for Arabic MT evaluation. Proceedings of the 2014 Conference on Empirical Methods in Natural Language Processing (EMNLP). http://dx.doi.org/10.3115/v1/d14-1026

Cho, K., van Merrienboer, B., Bahdanau, D., & Bengio, Y. (2014). On the properties of neural machine translation: Encoder–Decoder approaches. Proceedings of SSST-8, Eighth Workshop on Syntax, Semantics and Structure in Statistical Translation. http://dx.doi.org/10.3115/v1/w14-4012

Cuong, H., & Sima'an, K. (2017). A survey of domain adaptation for statistical machine translation. Machine Translation, 31(4), 187–224. https://doi.org/10.1007/s10590-018-9216-8

Darwish, A. (2009). Terminology and translation: A phonological-semantic approach to Arabic terminology. Writescope Publishers.

Dugonik, J., Sepesy Maučec, M., Verber, D., & Brest, J. (2023). Reduction of neural machine translation failures by incorporating statistical machine translation. Mathematics, 11(11), 2484. https://doi.org/10.3390/math11112484

El Marouani, M., Boudaa, T., & Enneya, N. (2020). Statistical error analysis of machine translation: The case of Arabic. Computación y Sistemas, 24(3). https://doi.org/10.13053/cys-24-3-3289

ElFqih, K. A., di Buono, M. P., & Monti, J. Towards a Linguistic Annotation of Arabic Legal Texts: A Multilingual Electronic Dictionary for Arabic. In Book of Abstracts (p. 17).

Gamal, D., Alfonse, M., Jimenez-Zafra, S. M., & Aref, M. (2022, May 8). Survey of Arabic machine translation, methodologies, progress, and challenges. 2022 2nd International Mobile, Intelligent, and Ubiquitous Computing Conference (MIUCC). http://dx.doi.org/10.1109/miucc55081.2022.9781776

Hadla, L., Taghreed, H., & Al-Kabi, M. (2014). Evaluating Arabic to English Machine Translation. International Journal of Advanced Computer Science and Applications, 5, 68–73. https://doi.org/10.14569/IJACSA.2014.051112#sthash.NW2l6vl5.dpuf

Halimi, S. A. (2017). Contextualizing translation decisions in legal system-bound and international multilingual contexts. Between Specialised Texts and Institutional Contexts – Competence and Choice in Legal Translation, 3(1), 20–46. https://doi.org/10.1075/ttmc.3.1.03hal

Han, L. (2016). Machine translation evaluation resources and methods: A survey. arXiv Preprint arXiv:1605.04515.

Haque, R., Hasanuzzaman, M., & Way, A. (2019). TermEval: An automatic metric for evaluating terminology translation in MT. Springer.

Haque, R., Hasanuzzaman, M., & Way, A. (2020). Analysing terminology translation errors in statistical and neural machine translation. Machine Translation, 34(2–3), 149–195. https://doi.org/10.1007/s10590-020-09251-z

Herold, C., Rosendahl, J., Vanvinckenroye, J., & Ney, H. (2022). Detecting various types of noise for neural machine translation. Findings of the Association for Computational Linguistics: ACL 2022. http://dx.doi.org/10.18653/v1/2022.findings acl.200

Izwaini, S. (2006). Problems of Arabic machine translation: evaluation of three systems. Proceedings of the International Conference on the Challenge of Arabic for NLP/MT, 118–148. https://aclanthology.org/2006.bcs-1.11

Junczys-Dowmunt, M., Dwojak, T., & Hoang, H. (2016). Is neural machine translation ready for deployment? A case study on 30 translation directions. arXiv Preprint arXiv:1610.01108.

Kalchbrenner, N., Grefenstette, E., & Blunsom, P. (2014). A convolutional neural network for modelling sentences. Proceedings of the 52nd Annual Meeting of the Association for Computational Linguistics (Volume 1: Long Papers). http://dx.doi.org/10.3115/v1/p14-1062

Khazin, K. M., Sanjaya, D., Siregar, M., Meisuri, & Adisaputra, A. (2023). Comparison of machine translations (MT) technology; statistical (SMT) vs. neural (NMT). ADVANCES IN FRACTURE AND DAMAGE MECHANICS XX. http://dx.doi.org/10.1063/5.0133311

Killman, J. (2014). Vocabulary accuracy of statistical machine translation in the legal context. Proceedings of the 11th Conference of the

Association for Machine Translation in the Americas, 85–98.

Koehn, P. (2020). Neural machine translation. Cambridge University Press.

Koehn, P., & Knowles, R. (2017). Six challenges for neural machine translation. Proceedings of the First Workshop on Neural Machine Translation. http://dx.doi.org/10.18653/v1/w17-3204

Koehn, P., Och, F. J., & Marcu, D. (2003). Statistical phrase-based translation. Defense Technical Information Center. http://dx.doi.org/10.21236/ada461156

Lavie, A., & Denkowski, M. J. (2009). The Meteor metric for automatic evaluation of machine translation. Machine Translation, 23(2–3), 105–115. https://doi.org/10.1007/s10590-009-9059-4

Lee, S., Lee, J., Moon, H., Park, C., Seo, J., Eo, S., Koo, S., & Lim, H. (2023). A Survey on Evaluation Metrics for Machine Translation. Mathematics, 11(4), 1006.

Madi, N., & Al-Khalifa, H. (2020). Error detection for Arabic text using neural sequence labeling. Applied Sciences, 10 (15), 5279. https://doi.org/10.3390/app10155279

Mediouni, M. (2016). Towards a functional approach to Arabic–english legal translation: The role of comparable/parallel texts. In M. Taibi (Ed.), New Insights into Arabic Translation and Interpreting (pp. 115–160). Multilingual Matters. http://dx.doi.org/10.21832/9781783095254-008

Müller, M., Rios, A., & Rico, S. (2019). Domain robustness in neural machine translation. arXiv Preprint arXiv:1911.03109.

Nishimura, T., & Akiba, T. (2017, August). Addressing unknown word problem for neural machine translation using distributee representations of words as input features. 2017 International Conference on Advanced Informatics, Concepts, Theory, and Applications (ICAICTA). http://dx.doi.org/10.1109/icaicta.2017.8090977

Papineni, K., Roukos, S., Ward, T., & Zhu, W. J. (2002). Bleu: a method for automatic evaluation of machine translation. Proceedings of the 40th Annual Meeting on Association for Computational Linguistics - ACL '02. http://dx.doi.org/10.3115/1073083.1073135

Rossi, C., & Carre, A. (2022). Machine translation for everyone: Empowering users in the age of artificial intelligence. Language Science Press Berlin, 18, 51. https://doi.org/10.5281/zenodo.6653406

Sager, J. C. (1990). Practical course in terminology processing. John Benjamins Publishing.

Sai, A. B., Mohankumar, A. K., & Khapra, M. M. (2022). A survey of evaluation metrics used for NLG systems. ACM Computing Surveys, 55(2), 1–39. https://doi.org/10.1145/3485766

Sepesy Maučec, M., & Donaj, G. (2019). Machine translation and the evaluation of its quality. In A. Sadollah & S. Tilendra (Eds.), Recent Trends in Computational Intelligence. IntechOpen. http://dx.doi.org/10.5772/intechopen.89063

Thierry, P. (2022). On" Human Parity" and" Super Human Performance" in Machine Translation Evaluation. Language Resource and Evaluation Conference.

Tiedemann, J. (2012). Parallel data, tools and interfaces in OPUS. Lrec, 2012, 2214–2217.

Vaswani, A., Shazeer, N., Parmar, N., Uszkoreit, J., Jones, L., Gomez, A. N., Kaiser, L., & Polosukhin, I. (2017, June 12). Attention is all you need. arXiv.Org. https://arxiv.org/abs/1706.03762

Vintar, Š. (2018). Terminology translation accuracy in statistical versus neural MT: An evaluation for the English-Slovene language pair. Proceedings of the Eleventh International Conference on Language Resources and Evaluation (LREC 2018), 34–37.

Wang, W., Tian, Y., Ngiam, J., Yang, Y., Caswell, I., & Parekh, Z. (2020). Learning a multi-domain curriculum for neural machine translation. Proceedings of the 58th Annual Meeting of the Association for Computational Linguistics. http://dx.doi.org/10.18653/v1/2020.acl-main.689

Silberztein, M. (2015). La formalisation des langues: l'approche de NooJ. ISTE Group.

Watson, D., Zalmout, N., & Habash, N. (2018). Utilizing character and word embeddings for text normalization with sequence-to-sequence models. Proceedings of the 2018 Conference on Empirical Methods in Natural Language Processing. http://dx.doi.org/10.18653/v1/d18-1097

Zakraoui, J., Saleh, M., Al-Maadeed, S., & AlJa'am, J. M. (2020, April). Evaluation of Arabic to English machine translation systems. 2020 11th International Conference on Information and Communication Systems (ICICS). http://dx.doi.org/10.1109/icics49469.2020.239518

Zakraoui, J., Saleh, M., Al-Maadeed, S., & Alja'am, J. M. (2021). Arabic machine translation: A survey with challenges and future directions. IEEE Access, 9, 161445–161468. https://doi.org/10.1109/access.2021.3132488

Ziemski, M., Junczys-Dowmunt, M., & Pouliquen, B. (2016). The United Nations parallel corpus v1. 0. Proceedings of the Tenth International Conference on Language Resources and Evaluation (LREC'16), 3530–3534.

Appendix

Table 3: Arabic Legal Documents

Documents	Type	Country	Tokens
Family Code	Code	Morocco	20,726
Code of Penal Procedures	Code	Morocco	76,945
Code of Obligations and Contracts	Code	Morocco	82,365
Civil Code	Code	Algeria	113,287
Penal Code		Algeria	113,287
Tunisian Code of Penal Status	Code	Tunisia	11,638
Code of Penal Procedures	Code	Tunisia	11,638
Qatari Civil Code	Code	Qatar	62,601
Constitution of the Kingdom of Morocco	Constitution	Morocco	12,494
Marriage Contract	Contract	Morocco	315
Real Estate Sale Contract	Contract	Algeria	427
Divorce by Mutual Consent before Marriage consummation	Provision	Morocco	277
Irrevocable Divorce after Marriage Consummation	Provision	Egypt	100
Irrevocable Divorce before Marriage Consummation	Provision	Egypt	131
Revocable divorce	Provision	Egypt	86
Self-divorce	Provision	Morocco	308
Total of Tokens			2148,981

Automatic Student Answer Assessment Using LSA

Teodora Mihajlov
University of Belgrade, Sebia
teodoramihajlov@gmail.com

Abstract

Implementing technology in a modern-day classroom is an ongoing challenge. In this paper, we created a system for an automatic assessment of student answers using Latent Semantic Analysis (LSA) – a method with an underlying assumption that words with similar meanings will appear in the same contexts. The system will be used within digital lexical flashcards for L2 vocabulary acquisition in a CLIL classroom. Results presented in this paper indicate that while LSA does well in creating semantic spaces for longer texts, it somewhat struggles with detecting topics in short texts. After obtaining LSA semantic spaces, answer accuracy was assessed by calculating the cosine similarity between a student's answer and the golden standard. The answers were classified by accuracy using the the K-Nearest Neighbor algorithm (KNN), for both binary and multinomial classification. The results of KNN classification are as follows: precision $P = 0.73$, recall $R = 1.00$, $F_1 = 0.85$ for binary classification, and $P = 0.50$, $R = 0.47$, $F_1 = 0.46$ score for the multinomial classifier. The results are to be taken with a grain of salt, due to a small test and training dataset.

1 Introduction

Employing technology to improve language learning outcomes is a problem scientists have wrestled with since the 1960s. In this paper, we present a beta version of a model for an automatic assessment of student answers using Latent Semantic Analysis (LSA) implemented in a use-case scenario, i.e. for assessing vocabulary knowledge of students and associates at the Faculty of Mining and Geology, University of Belgrade. In further development, the aim is for the model will be implemented within digital lexical flashcards for learning vocabulary in English as a Second Language (ESL) classes.

Previous research (Landauer et al., 1998; Lemaire and Dessus, 2003; Lifchitz et al., 2009) shows that many cognitive abilities in humans, including vocabulary acquisition, are well-represented by LSA. Furthermore, assessments provided by LSA largely correlated with those done by evaluators (Landauer et al., 1997; Graesser et al., 2000; Lemaire and Dessus, 2003; Landauer et al., 2003; Picca et al., 2015). Flashcards have proven to be a good tool for L2 vocabulary acquisition, combining interval (Ashcroft et al., 2018) and conscious learning (Nation, 2006; Hung, 2015) —- two approaches that enhance learning outcomes, especially at the lower levels of language knowledge (Ashcroft et al., 2018). In this phase of work, we will tackle several methodological problems, such as using LSA on short text, and finding means to contribute to the digitalisation of L2 classroom at the Faculty of Mining and Geology, University of Belgrade.

The research aims to examine the current general and geological vocabulary knowledge of the Faculty's students and associates and to improve teaching methods at the Faculty by utilising Natural Language Processing (NLP). Also, we examine LSA's application in the geological domain, and on shorter text, i.e. definitions. Conforming to the aforementioned aims, our hypotheses are: (1) the creation of the system will help digitalise learning materials; (2) LSA will be successful in assessing student answers.

The paper is organised as follows: in Section 2 we will go through previos research of vocabulary acqusition and LSA implementation in educaiton technologies, proceeding to data and model description in Section 3. After that, we will analyse the results in Section 4, starting from testng LSA model validity (Section 4.1) and going thorugh topic distribution (Section 4.2), and finishing with answer assessment (Section 4.3) and classification

Proceedings of the First ConTenNTS Workshop and the 16th BUCC workshop, pages 36–44
Varna, Sep 7, 2023
https://doi.org/10.26615/978-954-452-090-8_005

(Section 4.4). Finally, we will present concluding remarks in 5 and end with the limitations of our approach.

2 Related Works

In exploring L2 acquisition, vocabulary acquisition is widely researched. It is considered that vocabulary learning has the best outcomes when combining spaced (or distributed/interval) learning with explicit learning. Spaced learning is learning in many small sessions increasing the breaks between each session (Nation, 2006), while explicit learning assumes that the student is aware of the learning process (Nation, 2006; Hung, 2015; Ma, 2009). As flashcards provide simultaneous explicit and interval learning, together with learning word form, meaning and use in context (Ma, 2009), they make a great learning tool. Several researches display that flashcards significantly enhance L2 vocabulary acquisition outcomes, especially at the lower levels of language knowledge (Spiri, 2008; Nakata, 2008; Hung, 2015; Averianova, 2015; Yüksel et al., 2022). Given that students who are non-native English speakers can enter university with different levels of language knowledge, using flashcards as a teaching tool can help students reach the necessary level of English to follow classes and learning materials. Our case is no different. One of the main problems in ESL classes at the Faculty of Mining and Geology, University of Belgrade emphasised in (Beko et al., 2015) is a low level of language knowledge at the beginning of studies. Beko et al. (2015) also points out that students have in finding a suitable learning method, and lack of translation of geological terminology to Serbian, which makes translational tasks even more difficult. Our model will be monolingual, so we will not address the last-mentioned issue.

Currently, the Faculty uses a variety of language tools, a thesaurus of geological terminology in Serbian and English, comprised of roughly 2800 words (Beko et al., 2015), and a digital mining terminology platform *RudOnto*.[1] Additionally, a system of flashcards *RGF Flashcards* was developed, using *Anki* and integrated into the Faculty's *Moodle* platform.[2]

The presented system of flashcards will be tailored to the learning materials and adapted to the CLIL methodology used in the Faculty's English 1-4 subjects. CLIL integrates learning content from a certain domain with language learning (Beko, 2013; Djerić, 2019; Baten et al., 2020), whereby C1 entry language knowledge is expected. Thus, flashcards could facilitate learning for students with lower levels of English and make following of the learning materials and classes easier.

In this stage of development of the flashcards system, we aimed to create a model for an automatic assessment of the semantic similarity of student answers and the golden standard. For that purpose, we exploited LSA — a theory and method for extraction and representation of word meaning in context, whereby statistical calculations are applied to a large text corpus (Landauer et al., 1997). Thus far, research has shown that LSA can broadly represent human cognitive abilities, such as vocabulary acquisition, word categorisation, discourse comprehension, and essay assessment (Landauer et al., 1998). LSA has hitherto been used for answer assessment, providing feedback, answering student questions, as well as assessing student essay accuracy and coherency, in several smart games. In the essay assessment task, it displayed a high degree of correlation with evaluator assessments (Landauer et al., 1997; Graesser et al., 2000; Lemaire and Dessus, 2003; Landauer et al., 2003; Dikli, 2006; Lafourcade and Zampa, 2009; Picca et al., 2015). In the light of previously said, we believe that the method is suitable for our task as well.

The idea of context-based representation of word meaning is by no means a new one in linguistic theory. Harris (1954) fist posed that elements of a language appear relative to one another. Later an automatic clustering-based algorithm for word sense disambiguation was presented by Schütze (1998), where a cluster consists of contextually similar occurrences of a word. Distributional semantics also transcended to computational linguistics, and model such as Latent Semantic Analysis (LSA) and Latent Dirichlet Allocation (LDA) were developed (Landauer et al., 1997; Blei et al., 2003). More recently, with the development of neural networks, models such as Word2vec have became increasingly popular in representing word meaning (Mikolov et al., 2013). However, in a case study presented in Altszyler et al. (2016), LSA outperformed Skip-gram model when the size of the corpora was reduced from medium to small.

[1] RudOnto thesaurus, accessed 20 May 2023
[2] Moodle, accessed 20 May 2023

3 Experimental Setup

3.1 Data

Data Collection The data is a mixture of long and short texts, which enabled us to compare the LSA's performance between the two. The parts of the data used are as follows: 1) **unit texts** from the English-language textbook in preparation for subjects English 1-4 at the Faculty of Mining and Geology, University of Belgrade; 2) **vocabulary** following each textbook unit - general vocabulary (663 words), geological vocabulary (280 words), minerals (18 words); 3) **participant answers** collected via Faculty's Moodle platform enhanced with HP5 extension.[3] The test was an adapted test battery presented in (Jhean-Larose et al., 2010) and was split into three groups with different examples. Some questions (e.g. question six) were adjusted to the research aims. The test was completed by 14 participants. The participants were associates from the faculty - professors and teaching assistants, with good knowledge of geological terminology in both Serbian and English. After the completion of the testing process, 451 answers were collected. For anonymity purposes, we created a unique numerical ID for each participant. After analysing the test results, and extracting only answered open-ended questions, 72 answers remained for the analysis. Some answers were omitted from the analysis due to an unclear and inconsistent output in Moodle results. The length of unit texts, vocabulary, and participant answers in tokens is 46 888, 14 051, 5505, respectively.

Selecting the Assessment Criteria First, all answers were manually checked and assessed by the evaluator. The criterion was the answers' similarity to the golden standard - a definition from the textbook vocabulary, as well as the evaluator's English language competency. Since our model does not take into account grammar and spelling, neither did the evaluator in the assessment process. However, spelling was checked and corrected using the Grammarly[4] tool prior to feeding data to the model.

The answers were graded on a scale from 1 to 5, where 1 was completely incorrect and 5 was a correct answer. Subsequently, all answers that scored 1 were labelled as incorrect, while the rest were labelled as correct. We opted for adding the two-category assessment due to the small size of the dataset because, during the classification, our model accuracy might not be well represented when classifying 72 answers into 5 categories.

Data Preprocessing Text preparation was conducted in accordance with methods found in the literature (Deerwester et al., 1990; Dikli, 2006; Lifchitz et al., 2009), which we adapted to our goals and our data. The first step in text preparation was text lemmatisation using *SpaCy* library.[5] After obtaining lemmatised text surrogates for each part of our data, we removed punctuation and special characters using regular expressions and changed text to lowercase. In addition, we removed Latin abbreviations and plurals from the vocabulary (e.g. *data sing. datum, hypothesis pl. hypotheses*). An example of text before and after preparation is displayed in Table 1. The examples are extracted from different texts.

3.2 Models

For developing our LSA model, as well as for the the K-Nearest Neighbor (KNN) classification algorithm, we used the *Scikit-Learn* Python library.[6]

First, we constructed a TF-IDF matrix, with documents in matrix rows, terms in matrix columns, and relative term frequencies in each of the documents in matrix cells (Jurafsky and Martin, 2023). Trying out options between 700 and 5000 terms, we opted for a 1000-dimension TF-IDF matrix for unit texts, with a minimal term frequency of 3, and a maximal frequency of 80% of documents. In this step, we also removed stop words, which were a concatenation of the NLTK[7] stop words for the English-language, and corpus-specific stop words (*km, km/h, mm, meter, yet, well,* etc.). Initially, the same TF-IDF parameters were applied to short texts as well but this gave poor results. Thus, we lowered the number of dimensions to 700 and minimal frequency to 1, and increased maximum frequency to 100% of documents, while the stop word list contained only definite and indefinite article — *a/an, the*.

Subsequently, we set the SVD parameters that were the same for all parts of the data. The number of topics was determined by examining the first 10 terms with the highest weights in order to determine an appropriate number of topics, we extracted 15 terms weights for each topic. Finally, we opted for 10 topics. Then, we assigned a name to each

[3]HP5 extension, accessed 22 May 2023
[4]Grammarly, last accessed 25 August 2023
[5]SpaCy library, accessed 22 May 2023
[6]Scikit-Learn library, accessed 22 May 2023
[7]NLTK library, accessed 22 May 2023

Original text	Processed text
Most people today are familiar with mineral water and the perennial debate, as to whether still or sparkling is better.	most people today be familiar with mineral water and the perennial debate as to whether still or sparkle be well
Groundwater stored in subterranean aquifers has always been extracted for human use through the digging of wells.	groundwater store in subterranean aquifer have always be extract for human use through the digging of well

Table 1: Processed text

topic based on the first 100 terms with the highest weights. Separate semantic spaces were created for unit texts, i.e. long texts, and word definitions and participant answers, i.e. short texts. The names of the topics and their respective terms can be found in Appendix A.

After obtaining topic vectors, we measured cosine similarities between all texts, and between all the answers, and extracted the most similar ones, to check the LSA model validity for both long and short text. Next, we calculated a final score for each answer as a mean of cosine similarity of answer A and: a) vector of the unit text in which the defined term appears; b) vector of the correct answer (*golden standard*); c) vector of the previously obtained most similar answer B. The higher the similarity score of document A and document B, the higher the connection between the documents (Rahutomo et al., 2012). Finally, the answers were classified by accuracy using KNN, for both binomial (*Correct / Incorrect*) and multinomial classification (Li et al., 2003; Peterson, 2009).

4 Results and Analysis

4.1 Testing Model Validity

In order to check LSA validity for long text, we computed cosine similarity between all unit texts, and then detected the most similar ones. For short text, we did the same with participant answers.

Analysing the results, the supposition is that latent topics in unit texts are well-detected and that the most similar texts indeed convey similar topics. This has proven to be true, so the text about Wagner's hypothesis which explains an assumption of the existence of Pangaea, has the highest similarity with a text about tectonic plates. Furthermore, a text about volcanology is closely matched to a text about igneous rocks (Table 2).

The similarity between answers spreads from about 0.7 to 0.9. Unlike with unit text, the model was somewhat inconsistent with detecting the most similar answers, for example, answers that do not share the same terms were evaluated as most similar. However, so were the answers to the same question that do share many terms, as well as answers to different questions that share the same terms, such as answers to questions *hydrological cycle*: *the representation of a continuous, circular movement of water through the atmosphere, where the physical state of water alters as it flows through the cycle* and *seabed*: *land at the bottom of the ocean* both containing terms *earth, ocean, surface* (Table 3).

Based on these results, we can argue that our model did better in detecting topics in longer texts than in short ones.

4.2 Topic Distribution

The highest standard deviation of topics was observed in unit texts, while it was somewhat lower in vocabulary and answers. We believe that the reason behind the lower standard deviation in vocabulary and answers is a more coherent text form compared to unit texts.

In unit texts, maximal topic values vary between 0.5617 in *Volcanology*, to 0.3638 in *Dating*, while minimal values fluctuate from 0.3878 for *EarthFormation*, all the way to -0.001 for topic *Dating*. Maximal values in definitions are, to a degree, more evenly distributed. Topic *Weathering* (0.7067) has the highest maximum value, while the lowers is that of *Landslides* (0.3547). Almost all minimal topic values are negative, apart from the topic *EarthFormation*, with a minimal value of 0.0193. While topics are assigned well to some geological terms, e.g. *debris* has high values in *EarhFormation, Weathering* and *Landslides*, the model failed to recognise latent topics in others, which is shown for exam-

Text A	Text B	Similarity
palaeozoic era	mesozoic era and cenozoic	0.9776
wegener s hypothesis	tectonic plates	0.8980
volcanoes	igneous rocks	0.8229
the causes of metamorphism	metamorphic textures	0.9606
coal as a fossil fuel	oil and natural gas mineral oil	0.7726

Table 2: Examples of the most similar texts

Text A	Text B	Similarity
hydrological cycle	seabed	0.8685
unconsolidate	backlash	0.0000
urbanisation	urbanisation	0.9840

Table 3: Examples of the most similar answers

ple in a low value of topic *Fossils* in definitions of terms *fossil, fossilised, fossilisation*. In participant answers, we find that the topic *TectonicPlates* has the highest maximal value (0.7042), while the lowest one is that of *Landslides*, with just 0.3612. Minimal values are for the most part negative, and have values between -0.5557 for Minerals and 0.0000 for *EarthFormation*. Answers to the same question mainly have similar topic distribution. Most answers to the question *global warming* have the highest values for the topic *EarthFormatoin*, and the lowest for *Erosion* and *Landslides*. All topic values for short, incomplete answers, consisting of just 1 or 2 words, are 0.

In all parts of the data, topic *EarthFormation* is the most frequent one, appearing in 34 out of 36 unit texts, and in most definitions and answers. The high frequency of this topic does not come as a surprise, as it contains vocabulary that is woven through most of the texts. Other frequent topics include *Volcanology*, *Weathering*, and *Landslides*, while the least frequent ones are *Minerals* and *Dating*. Relative frequencies of all topic, as well as values of the dominant topic for the first 30 data points in all parts of the data are displayed in Figure 1.

4.3 Answer Assessment

After analysing topic distribution, we proceed to assess the participant answers, by the criteria explained in 3.2. The lowest value in the final score is 0, which is the score of previously explained very short answers (1-2 words), while long answers show little variance between the three values used for computing the final score.

As displayed in Table 4, some correct answers have lower similarity with the corresponding unit texts than incorrect answers, and the final score of correct and incorrect answers is relatively similar. This raises the question if our method should be revised. To a human evaluator, a similarity difference of 0.1 might be significant when they look at the broader picture, but we will see if that will be the case with our classification model as well.

In a two-category distribution, the final score has lower values in correct than in incorrect answers, and values of correct answers have a greater range. In the five-grade answer assessment, we can see that values of answers graded 2 are most scattered, while the densest ones are those of answers with grade 1, and higher grades have relatively similar final scores.

Cosine similarity of the most similar answers probability greatly contributed to high values of incorrect answers, since only the highest similarity values were taken into account. Furthermore, answer accuracy was best represented by the cosine similarity between an answer and a golden standard (correct answer). Nonetheless, we opted for keeping the previously determined final score computation, because we wanted to see how the model does in comparing long and short text. Another reason behind this is that the description of a term in unit text and its respective definition in the unit vocabulary can slightly differ, f.x. the description of a geological term in the unit text could be longer, or synonyms can be used. Since synonyms will rarely appear together, we thought this might be a way to overcome this obstacle. In further research, extracting only the sentences of unit texts actually explaining a certain geological notion might be the solution. Additionally, high weights of functional

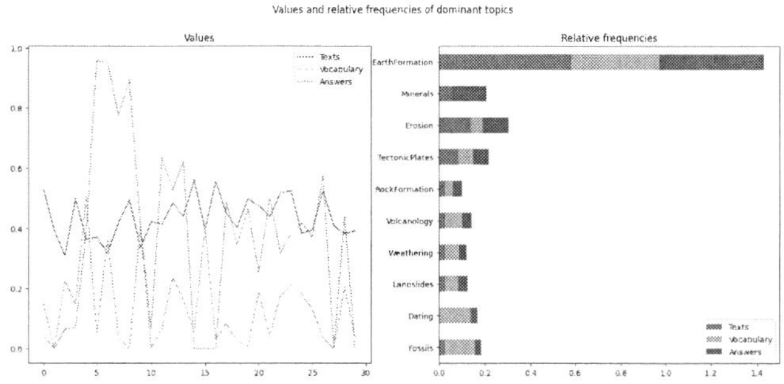

Figure 1: Dominant topics values in vocabulary

QID	PID	Answer A	Text	Def.	Answer B	Final Score	C/I	1-5
3	3	convergent	0.0000	0.2885	0.9992	0.7354	C	4
3	4	convergent	-0.3299	0.2999	0.9992	0.7377	I	1
8	3	straightforward	-0.0291	0.0011	0.9627	0.6807	I	1

Table 4: Final answer score; QID – question ID, participant ID, C/I – Correct/Incorrect, 1-5 – grade on a scale from 1 to 5

words in the semantic space of definitions and answer topics (*be, of, in, to, or, by*, etc.) might have contributed to the results. In future work, we could solve this by removing functional words with high weights from definitions and answers, and see if the results improve.

4.4 Answer Classification

The final step was a multinomial and binary answer classification. For classification purposes KNN algorithm was employed (Li et al., 2003; Peterson, 2009; Chen, 2018), labels corresponded with the evaluator assessment, while the classification criteria was the final answer score. Recall, precision and F_1 score were used for evaluation (Géron, 2022).

In binary classification, answers were classified as correct or incorrect. The data is comprised of 60 correct and 12 incorrect answers. Due to this discrepancy, the model classified all answers as correct. Calculated model precision was 73%, recall 100%, and $F_1 = 0.85$. The size of our data might have affected the performance of the classification algorithm, given that our data set is rather small, containing only 72 observations, consequently so is the test set with mere 15 observations. Since the data is randomly split into a training and test set, it can just so happen that all the observations in the test set have the same label.

In the multinomial classification, category frequency is uneven. Consequently, the model did poorly in classifying the underrepresented categories, i.e. grades 1 (incorrect) and 5 (completely correct). For the multinomial classification, model parameters are as follows: precision was 50%, recall 47% and $F_1 = 0.46$. Since the model was classifying mere 15 answers into 5 categories with uneven distribution in the data, it is expected that the results are worse than those of binary classification.

5 Conclusion

In this paper, we discussed the application of Latent Semantic Analysis for the assessment of short answers. In accordance with the set pedagogical goals of this paper, we extrapolated that the utilisation of flashcards for L2 vocabulary acquisition gives favourable results, particularly at the lower levels of language knowledge. As students of the Faculty of Mining and Geology come from different educational backgrounds and usually enter their studies with a low level of English, we strongly believe that using a system of flashcards that accompany the subject textbook would greatly help students to make progress faster and get to a level of vocabulary knowledge suitable for following CLIL lectures.

Reflecting on the methodological aims of the paper, we determined that developing this model helped us recognise the advantages and disadvantages of our approach. One of the greatest advantages of the model is good topic modelling of longer texts and vocabulary and answers pertaining to geology. We deem that the biggest downside is its inability to detect topics of very short answers.

To overcome model downsides, the first step in further research would be to expand the answer data set. Our second goal is to add a system for spelling and grammar assessment. In order to improve the results obtained using LSA, we could try and lower the number of dimensions. Additionally, creating separate semantic spaces for words that are not geological notions, i.e. general vocabulary, might be a good idea. When comparing answers and unit texts, we believe that we would get more meaningful results if we extract just a fragment of the text where a certain geological notion is explained or a word belonging to the general vocabulary used. Lastly, instead of computing the similarity of all answers, we would proceed to calculate the similarity of answers to the same question.

The presented model development laid a foundation for the development of a system for automatic answer assessment in digital flashcards. Comparing the goals and aims of CLIL methodology and the outcomes of using flashcards in teaching, we concluded that this technology would greatly complement the textbook in preparation. Our claim is supported by the Faculty's students' positive attitude towards using digital flashcards in an L2 classroom expressed in previous research. Ultimately, we intend to accomplish the project's main goal — the development of a digital flashcard system that will be implemented in the classroom.

Limitations

The main limitation of work presented in this paper is a small data set. Not only did scarce data made it more difficult to find the right parameters for creating semantic spaces, but it also hindered the classification task. Additionally, feature extraction in short texts, i.e. definitions and answers, should be revised. By removing just articles, we left too much noise in these parts of the data, which resulted in topics having similar terms with the highest weights. Methodologically, the biggest downside, in our opinion, is a lack of demographic questionnaire, where the participants would fill out their English language levels, by either self-evaluation, or state if they possess an English language certificate, as well as their age, gender and professional qualification. This should be included in further research. Having the level of participants knowledge would have provided us with an additional criteria for LSA assessment, but also help us make conclusions on the needs of our user target group.

Acknowledgements

This paper is a result of Master thesis at the Social Sciences and Computing MSc program at the University of Belgrade. The author would hereby like to thank their mentor prof. Dr Ranka Stanković for her help and advice, as well as prof. Dr Lidija Beko, for landing her textbook in preparation for the purposes of this work.

References

Edgar Altszyler, Mariano Sigman, Sidarta Ribeiro, and Diego Fernández Slezak. 2016. Comparative study of lsa vs word2vec embeddings in small corpora: a case study in dreams database. *arXiv preprint arXiv:1610.01520.*

Robert John Ashcroft, Robert Cvitkovic, and Max Praver. 2018. Digital flashcard l2 vocabulary learning out-performs traditional flashcards at lower proficiency levels: A mixed-methods study of 139 japanese university students. *The EuroCALL Review*, 26(1):14–28.

Irina Averianova. 2015. Vocabulary acquisition in l2: does call really help. In *Critical CALL–Proceedings of the 2015 EUROCALL Conference, Padova, Italy*, pages 30–35.

Kristof Baten, Silke Van Hiel, and Ludovic De Cuypere. 2020. Vocabulary development in a clil context: A comparison between french and english l2. *Studies in second language learning and teaching*, 10(2):307–336.

Lidija Beko. 2013. *Integrisano učenje sadržaja i jezika (CLIL) na geološkim studijama.* Phd thesis, Univerzitet u Beogradu, Filološki fakultet.

Lidija Beko, Ivan Obradović, and Ranka Stanković. 2015. Developing students' mining and geology vocabulary through flashcards and l1 in the clil classroom. In *The Second International Conference on Teaching English for Specific Purposes Developing students' mining and geology vocabulary through flashcards and L1 in the CLIL classroom.* Faculty of Electronic Engineering, University of Niš.

David M Blei, Andrew Y Ng, and Michael I Jordan. 2003. Latent dirichlet allocation. *Journal of machine Learning research*, 3(Jan):993–1022.

Shufeng Chen. 2018. K-nearest neighbor algorithm optimization in text categorization. In *IOP conference series: earth and environmental science*, volume 108, page 052074. IOP Publishing.

Scott C. Deerwester, Susan T. Dumais, Thomas K. Landauer, George W. Furnas, and Richard A. Harshman. 1990. Indexing by latent semantic analysis. *Journal of the American Society for Information Science*, 41:391–407.

Semire Dikli. 2006. An overview of automated scoring of essays. *Journal of Technology, Learning, and Assessment*, 5(1).

Miloš Djerić. 2019. Doprinos clil-a savremenim tokovima nastave stranog jezika. *Philologia*, 17(17):23–38. 3.

Aurélien Géron. 2022. *Hands-on machine learning with Scikit-Learn, Keras, and TensorFlow*. O'Reilly Media, Inc.

Arthur Graesser, Peter Wiemer-Hastings, Katja Wiemer-Hastings, Derek Harter, Natalie Person, and Tutoring Research Group. 2000. Using latent semantic analysis to evaluate the contributions of students in autotutor. *Interactive Learning Environments*, 8:129–148.

Zellig S Harris. 1954. Distributional structure. *Word*, 10(2-3):146–162.

Hsiu-Ting Hung. 2015. Intentional vocabulary learning using digital flashcards. *English Language Teaching*, 8:107–112.

Sandra Jhean-Larose, Vincent Leclercq, Javier Diaz, Guy Denhiere, and Bernadette Bouchon-Meunier. 2010. Knowledge evaluation based on lsa : Mcqs and free answers. *Stud. Inform. Univ.*, 8:57–84.

Daniel Jurafsky and James Martin. 2023. *Speech and Language Processing: An Introduction to Natural Language Processing, Computational Linguistics, and Speech Recognition*, 3 edition, volume 2. Draft of January 7, 2023.

Mathieu Lafourcade and Virginie Zampa. 2009. Pticlic: a game for vocabulary assessment combining jeuxdemots and lsa. In Alexander Gelbuch, editor, *Advances in Computational Linguistics*, volume 41, pages 289–298. Center for Computing Research of IPN.

Thomas Landauer, Darreil Laham, and Peter Foltz. 2003. Automated scoring and annotation of essays with the intelligent essay assessor. In Mark D. Shermis and Jill C. Burstein, editors, *Automated essay scoring: A cross-disciplinary perspective*, pages 87–112. Routledge.

Thomas K. Landauer, Peter W. Foltz, and Laham Darrell. 1998. An introduction to latent semantic analysis. *Discourse Processes*, 25(2–3):259–284.

Thomas K Landauer, Darrell Laham, Bob Rehder, and Missy E Schreiner. 1997. How well can passage meaning be derived without using word order? a comparison of latent semantic analysis and humans. In *Proceedings of the 19th annual meeting of the Cognitive Science Society*, pages 412–417.

Benoit Lemaire and Philippe Dessus. 2003. A system to assess the semantic content of student essays. *Journal of Educational Computing Research*, 24.

Baoli Li, Shiwen Yu, and Qin Lu. 2003.

Alain Lifchitz, Sandra Jhean-Larose, and Guy Denhière. 2009. Effect of tuned parameters on an lsa multiple choice questions answering model. *Behavior research methods*, 41:1201–1209.

Qing Ma. 2009. *Second language vocabulary acquisition*, volume 79. Peter Lang.

Tomas Mikolov, Ilya Sutskever, Kai Chen, Greg Corrado, and Jeffrey Dean. 2013. Distributed representations of words and phrases and their compositionality.

Tatsuya Nakata. 2008. English vocabulary learning with word lists, word cards and computers: Implications from cognitive psychology research for optimal spaced learning. *ReCALL*, 20(1):3–20.

Paul Nation. 2006. *Vocabulary: Second Language*, pages 448–454.

Leif E Peterson. 2009. K-nearest neighbor. *Scholarpedia*, 4(2):1883.

Davide Picca, Dominique Jaccard, and Gérald Eberlé. 2015. Natural language processing in serious games: a state of the art. *International Journal of Serious Games*, 2(3):77–97.

Faisal Rahutomo, Teruaki Kitasuka, and Masayoshi Aritsugi. 2012. Semantic cosine similarity. In *The 7th international student conference on advanced science and technology ICAST*, volume 4.

Hinrich Schütze. 1998. Automatic word sense discrimination. *Computational Linguistics*, 24(1):97–123.

John Spiri. 2008. Online study of frequency list vocabulary with the wordchamp website. *Reflections on English Language Teaching*, 7(1):21–36.

H. Gülru Yüksel, H. Güldem Mercanoğlu, and M. Betül Yılmaz. 2022. Digital flashcards vs. wordlists for learning technical vocabulary. *Computer Assisted Language Learning*, 35(8):2001–2017.

Appendices

A Appendix

Topic	Name	Terms with the highest weights
Topic0	Earth Formation	mineral, cycle, earth, deposit, flow, sedimentary, igneous, material, soil, metamorphic
Topic1	Minerals	mineral, metamorphism, grain, metamorphic, igneous, metamorphic rock, pressure, crystal, magma, ore
Topic2	Erosion	flow, soil, particle, stream, slope, erosion, debris, landslide, glacial, material
Topic3	Tectonic Plates	plate, earthquake, wave, cycle, tectonic, magma, continental, oceanic, magnetic, magnetic field
Topic4	Rock Formation	sedimentary, cycle, sediment, metamorphic, igneous, sedimentary rock, strata metamorphic rock, metamorphism, erosion
Topic5	Volcanology	magma, lava, grain, volcano, slope, eruption, volcanic, viscosity, period, landslide
Topic6	Weathering	wave, earthquake, magnetic, date, particle, magnetic field, metamorphism, stress, erosion, sediment
Topic7	Landslides	slope, landslide, soil, debris, hazard, cycle, trigger, activity, fall, downslope
Topic8	Dating	earth, strata, magma, date, age, eruption, lava, idea, satellite, remote
Topic9	Fossils	oil, wave, earthquake, coal, trap, organic, sedimentary, sedimentary rock, weathering, carbon

Semantic Specifics of Bulgarian Verbal Computer Terms

Maria A. Todorova
Institute For Bulgarian Language, Bulgarian Academy of Sciences,
Sofia, Bulgaria
maria@dcl.bas.bg

Abstract

This paper represents a description of Bulgarian verbal computer terms with a view to the specifics of their translation in English. The study employs a subset of 100 verbs extracted from the Bulgarian WordNet (BulNet) and from the internet. The analysis of their syntactic and semantic structure is a part of a study of the general lexis of Bulgarian. The aim of the paper is to (1) identify some problem areas of the description and translation of general lexis verbs, (2) offer an approach to the semantic description of metaphor-based terms from the perspective of Frame Semantics; (3) raise questions about the definition of general lexis with respect to Bulgarian and across languages.

1 Introduction

This paper aims at a conceptual description of high-frequency Bulgarian verbs from the domain of computer terminology as compared with English, with some implications about the conceptual description of the relevant verbs. The goal of the analysis is to contribute both to the enrichment of the Bulgarian WordNet with Conceptual frames (Koeva, 2020) and to the enlargement of the Bulgarian FrameNet, and hence — to the creation of a linked semantic and syntactic resource.

WordNet and FrameNet are large lexical resources that provide semantic information about verb classes. WordNet (Fellbaum, 1999) represents a multilingual conceptual network of synonym sets (synsets) linked by means of semantic relations such as hypernymy, antonymy, etc. FrameNet (Baker et al., 1998) represents the semantics of lexemes by means of schematic representations (frames) describing objects, situations, or events and their components (frame elements) in the apparatus of Frame Semantics.

The hypothesis adopted in this work is that some of the term-specific words which are encountered in everyday language use belong to a semantic field (Clark, 1993) recognised as part of the general lexis.

The proposed analyses are based on the general verb lexis of Bulgarian selected for the purposes of the theoretical semantic description and typology of verb predicates belonging to the basic conceptual apparatus of the language[1] (Leseva et al., 2021; Todorova et al., 2022; Todorova, 2023). The paper also discusses some problems of domain-specific semantic representation in terms of semantic fields (Clark, 1993), abstract meaning representation of metaphor-based terms and their translation into English using WordNet as a bilingual Bulgarian - English dictionary.

The study would help to (1) identify some problem areas of the description and translation of general lexis verbs, (2) offer an approach to the semantic description of metaphor-based terms from the perspective of Frame Semantics; (3) raise questions about the definition of general lexis with respect to both Bulgarian and other languages.

The remainder of the paper is organised as follows. Section 2 describes the data used in the study – a set of computer verb terms excerpted from WordNet, a selection of manually collected verbs from the internet and a set of semantic frames. Section 3 presents the semantic features of the verb set and a comparison of the semantic descriptions of computer term verbs and their literal, non-terminological counterparts. Section 4 discusses the semantic features of the combinations of general lexis verbs and noun computer terms resulting in verb-headed computer terms. Section 5 sums up the observations on the results and suggests directions for future work.

[1]The selection and evaluation of the verbs that form the set of the general lexis of Bulgarian has been undertaken by the team of linguists at the Department of Computational Linguistics of the Institute for Bulgarian Language at the Bulgarian Academy of Sciences.

Proceedings of the First ConTenNTS Workshop and the 16th BUCC workshop, pages 45–50
Varna, Sep 7, 2023
https://doi.org/10.26615/978-954-452-090-8_006

2 General Lexis and Computer Terms

It is considered that the volume of information that humanity creates and manages doubles every ten years, while the information in the area of telecommunications doubles every year. The mass penetration of telecommunications in all areas of human activity, including households has led to the demand of relatively good telecommunication literacy skills in anyone, even children. The prevalence of technology in daily life and education, along with media influence, and the overall social prestige of technological adoption results in the integration of computer terms into everyday vocabulary. Many computer terms have become so widely-used that they have entered the general vocabulary of languages. These terms are often used by people who may not have deep technical knowledge but are familiar with basic technology concepts. Words like *browse* or *click* have become as common as *iron* or *play*.

The study of verbs in the field of terminology with respect to Bulgarian has been focused mainly on the creation of new lexis (Blagoeva, 2007; Kostova, 2015) or on aspects of the metaphorical meaning of such terms (Kirova, 2018). Previous research in this field has approached the semantic description of terminological units from the perspective of Frame-based Terminology (Faber, 2012, 2015). However, this theory has not been implemented for the domain of telecommunications or Bulgarian terminology.

3 The Data Analysed

The computer terms were extracted from a bilingual terminological database representing 729 terms from the Computer and Technology domain in English and their translation equivalents in Bulgarian. The database[2] was created within the framework of the European Language Resource Coordination (ELRC) Connecting Europe Facility – Automated Translation (CEF.AT), Actions SMART 2014/1074 and SMART 2015/1091. The terminological resource has been compiled by combining the relevant entries in the Bulgarian WordNet – BulNet (Koeva, 2010) and entries in some other terminological monolingual dictionaries and domain-specific corpora. 319 of the terms were selected as candidates for the set of everyday lexis based on (1) the inclusion of their verb head as part of a previously selected set of general lexis verb literals in BulNet; (2) the availability of a term in the Dictionary of neologisms[3]; and (3) the frequency of the verb in the Bulgarian National Corpus (Koeva et al., 2012). As a result, 200 nouns, 110 verbs and 9 adverbs, representing the domain of information and technology in everyday life, were extracted. As the database represents the use of the selected computer terms since 2014 and their actual use nowadays, I assume that they have been firmly established in the language as part of a stable semantic field within the general lexis set.

The descriptions of lexical semantics of verb terms are based on the combined information from the following language resources: WordNet (Fellbaum, 1999), FrameNet (Ruppenhofer et al., 2016) and the mapping of FrameNet frames and WordNet synsets (Stoyanova and Leseva, 2020).

4 Semantic Features

4.1 Semantic grouping based on semantic primitives

In order to characterise the semantic field of common computer terminology, I use the semantic domains of the verbs extracted from WordNet. These domains are grouped in 15 lexicographer's files in WordNet (Miller et al., 1990). The selected verbs are mainly from the semantic domains of verbs of contact, verbs of communication, verbs of motion, and verbs of possession.

- **Verbs of communication** refer to actions involving the exchange, transmission, and interaction of information and data between users, devices, or systems: *izprashtam* (send)[4]; *poluchavam* (receive); *prenasyam* (transfer); *spodelyam* (share); *svarzvam se* (connect); *otgovaryam* (reply).

- **Verbs of motion** describe actions related to the management, transfer, and manipulation of data and files: *kopiram* (copy); *shtrakvam klikvam* (click); *premestvam* (move); *iztrivam* (delete); *postavyam* (paste);*pridarpvam* (drag); *puskam* (drop); *otvaryam* (open); *zatvaryam* (close).

- **Verbs of possession** relate to actions involving ownership, control, and access to digital

[2]available online on `https://data.europa.eu/data/datasets/elrc_312?locale=en`

[3]available online on `https://ibl.bas.bg/infolex/neologisms.php`

[4]The Bulgarian examples transliterated in the Latin script are followed by their translation equivalents

resources and data: *ogranichavam* (restrict); *zaklyuchvam* (lock); *spodelyam* (share); *zapazvam* (save).

- **Verbs of physical contact** refer to actions involving the manipulation, operation, and interaction with hardware or devices: *natiskam* (press); *plazgam* (swipe); *razlistvam* (scroll); *vmakvam* (insert); *prikachvam* (attach); *otpechatvam* (print).

The general semantics of these groups corresponds to Conceptual frames. Most of the selected verbs have non-terminological verb counterparts. Their terminological meaning is based on metaphorical transfer which may lead to ambiguity or wrong translations. This is where the role of their description by means of semantic frames and the specification of the semantic frames of non-terminological verbs comes into play.

4.2 Semantic Frames

The description of the selected verbs by means of semantic frames and the representation of their semantic features – i.e. their frame elements and the relevant semantic restrictions – has been undertaken as part of the description of Conceptual frames in Bulgarian. Conceptual frames are abstract structures that describe particular types of situations or events, along with their participants and properties (Koeva, 2020). The semantic specialisation occurring within a semantic class may result in different configurations of frame elements across frames, including the inclusion or exclusion of elements, the narrowing down of their semantics (stricter selectional restrictions), etc.

Verbs in the domain of verbal computer terms refer to actions or processes involving interaction, communication and connection in the digital and technological context. The semantic field of computer terms involves a general conceptualisation of situations represented by a set of common core frame elements which may vary depending on the specific term and its context:

Agent: The entity that initiates or performs the action: a user, a device, a system, or a programme.

Theme: The entity or object which is affected by the action: a file, e-mail, a device, a network, or a system resource.

Source: The location or entity from which data originate in the cases of data transfer or movement: a computer or a server.

Destination: The location or entity to which data are transferred or sent to: a computer or a server.

Medium: A physical input device, software interface, network connection, etc.

Result: The outcome or consequence of the action.

Depending on the particular verbs only the relevant frame elements are used to describe the concept. They are additionally specified by the sectional restrictions (represented in terms of semantic classes of nouns).

For example, the semantic frame of the verb *send* within the context of communication technologies is a specification of the FrameNet frame ***Sending***[5] – and captures the core concepts related to the act of transmitting information or data from one location to another, which includes the following frame elements: an **Agent** – an entity which is a user, a programme or a device; a **Source** – the location or entity from which the data or information originates; a **Destination** – the location or entity to which the data or information is being transmitted; and a **Content** – the information, data, or message that is being sent from the **Source** to the **Destination**.

4.3 Verbal Computer Terms vs. Their Non-computer Counterparts

Verbal computer terms often share similarities with their non-computer counterparts in terms of argument structure. This allows the use of the WordNet hierarchy and its mapping with FrameNet to suggest the corresponding frame. After an appropriate frame is selected, further specify the relevant frame elements with a view to the domain of technology and telecommunications. In this way, the WordNet structure is used to enrich and make more specific the FrameNet hierarchy. However, there can be differences due to the technical nature of computing concepts and the specific actions they describe. Here are a few examples comparing computer-related terms with their non-computer counterparts.

For example, the verbs *svalyam (download)* vs. *izvlicham (retrieve)*, both described by the FrameNet frame ***Removing***, differ mainly in the semantic restrictions imposed on the frame elements. The semantic frame of *svalyam (download)* is represented by an **Agent** – realised as the subject and defined as a user or a system performing the action, and a **Theme** – realised as the object and

[5] `https://framenet.icsi.berkeley.edu/`

defined as the data or files being transferred from a Source.The **Source** is a Location which is an adjunct of the verb and is defined as a server or a cloud from which the data is obtained.
Example: She downloaded the file from the Internet.
The semantic frame of *izvlicham (retrieve)* is represented by an **Agent** – realised as the subject and defined as a **Person** performing the action, and a **Theme** – realised as the object and defined as an **Item** being obtained. The **Source** is an adjunct of the verb and is defined as the location or origin of the **Item**.
Example: It took him some time to retrieve the file from the system. In addition, there are noun terms in the domain of computer technology which are presented in the argument structure of verbs belonging to the general lexis which do not have specialised meaning on their own. The combination of the non-terminological verb and the terminological noun results has terminological meaning itself. For example in the sentence, I'm using a mouse and headphones – the verb does not belong to the field of technology, only its arguments are computer terms. This shows specialised argument selection in the thematic domain under study and specialised use of general lexis verbs, which may pose problems to their translation via computer-aided tools.

4.4 Translation and Metaphors

As metaphors involve the use of a word or a phrase to describe an object or concept by comparing it to another object or concept, they play a role in enriching and expanding the general lexis of a language. Metaphors allow speakers to express abstract or complex ideas in terms of familiar and concrete concepts. Many computer term metaphors have become so deeply embedded in the language that they have lost their figurative meanings in the consciousness of speakers. People use them without recognising their metaphorical origin. In the context of digital technology, metaphors have significantly impacted general lexis. Many verbal computer terms such as *send, paste, open, close* etc. have been losing the transparency relation with their non-figurative counterparts. This is especially true for noun computer terms such as *window, virus, path, net, menu*, etc. Metaphors in the context of technology help bridge the gap between unfamiliar concepts and everyday experiences, making the terminology more accessible and relatable.

4.5 Translation and Adaptation

Though the set of computer terms studied in this paper belong to the specialised semantic field of computer technology, they represent a borderline case of terminological/ non-terminological lexis. In addition, they do not represent word-to-word correspondences, and a verbatim rendition in another language may lead to wrong word-to-word translation.
Most of the entries in the set of selected computer term verbs are common domestic words corresponding to the relevant English computer term. Such examples are represented by pairs such as *kachvam – upload, svalyam – download,* which are not terminological correspondences. This may lead to their non-terminological translation in English by another meaning of the Bulgarian verb, e.g. *kachvam – climb, ssvalyam – put down.*
Some computer terms – borrowed foreign words have been translated or adapted to fit the linguistic patterns of the Bulgarian language(Blagoeva, 2007). This adaptation makes the terms more accessible to a wider audience with the help of domestic word-formation means employed in previously adopted loan words. For example, the English term *click* has yielded the verb *klikvam*. The word has another orthographic correspondence in Bulgarian, meaning a distance in army terminology. This raises another ambiguity problem for translation technologies.
There are also some examples of literalisation of English metaphorical terms, mainly nouns and adjectives, through their translation in Bulgarian, consider the English term *free* (software) and *bezplaten* (i.e. 'non-paid') softuer. The classes of metaphorised common lexis verbs are described in more detail by Kirova (Kirova, 2018). Determining the appropriate translation strategies of such verbs, is necessary for eliminating ambiguities and different interpretations in computer-assisted text analysis.

5 Discussion

One of the main points of discussions in this paper is whether computer terms used in the everyday language contribute to the general lexis. These terms have become so integrated into modern communication that they are often used in everyday conversations, even by individuals who might not consider themselves tech-savvy. As technology continues

to play a significant role in our lives, these terms are likely to become even more ingrained in the common vocabulary.
Another interesting problem rooting from the question of the place of abstract words in the general lexis set is whether metaphor-based terms are part of it.

6 Conclusions

This study presents a dataset of Bulgarian – English verbal computer terms from a semantic point of view which takes into account their role as a part of the relevant semantic field in the general lexis of Bulgarian. They demonstrate the integration of computer terms into everyday language and their translation and the dynamic relationship between language and technology as a result of the evolving nature of human communication. As Bulgarian is a less-resourced language, the dataset might contribute to the implementation of domain-specific tasks in computer-assisted human translation from and to this language.
Computer terms of metaphorical origin enrich the general lexis of a language and contribute to the language's evolution and the way we understand and communicate complex ideas, including those related to digital technology. The semantic description of words specific to a particular semantic field, in this case computer terms, is a specification of the semantic description of their non-terminological, non-metaphorical counterparts.
As the proposed analysis is based on interlinked multilingual language resources (WordNet and FrameNet), the observations may also be useful for other languages and may contribute to the implementation of NLP applications aimed at automatic semantic analysis, word sense disambiguation, language understanding and generation, machine translation, etc.

Acknowledgments

The research presented in this paper is carried out as part of the scientific programme under the project *Enriching the Semantic Network WordNet with Semantic Frames* funded by the Bulgarian National Science Fund (Grant Agreement No. KP-06-N50/1 of 2020).

References

C. F. Baker, Ch.J. Fillmore, and John B. Lowe. 1998. The berkeley framenet project. *COLINGACL '98: Proceedings of the Conference. Montreal, Canada*, pages 86–90.

D. Blagoeva. 2007. Neologizmite v savremennia balgarski ezik. *Elektronno spisanie LiterNet*, 2.

Eve V. Clark. 1993. *The Lexicon in Acquisition*. Cambridge University Press.

P. Faber. 2012. A cognitive linguistics view of terminology andspecialized language.

P. Faber. 2015. Frames as a framework for terminology. *Kockaert, Hendrik J. and Frieda Steurs (eds.), Handbook of Terminology*, pages 14–33.

C. Fellbaum. 1999. The organization of verbs and verb concepts in a semantic net. *Text, Speech and Language Technology*, 6:278–301.

L. Kirova. 2018. Kompyutarna leksika, poluchena chrez metaforichen prenos na znachenieto na obshtoupotrebimi dumi. *Elektronno spisanie Liternet*.

S. Koeva. 2010. Bulgarian wordnet - current state, applications and prospects. *Bulgarian-American Dialogues*, pages 120–132.

S. Koeva. 2020. Towards a semantic network enriched with a variety of semantic relations. *Semantic Relations and Conceptual Frames, Koeva, S. (ed.)*, pages 7–20.

S. Koeva, I. Stoyanova, S. Leseva, T. Dimitrova, R. Dekova, and E. Tarpomanova. 2012. The Bulgarian National Corpus: Theory and practice in corpus design. *Journal of Language Modelling*, pages 65–110.

N. Kostova. 2015. Verb neologisms and respective names for actions in bulgarian language. *Balgarski ezik*, 62:48–57.

S. Leseva, I. Stoyanova, M. Todorova, and H. Kukova. 2021. Putting pieces together: Predicate-argument relations and selectional preferences. *Koeva, S. (ed.) Towards a Semantic Network Enriched with a Variety of Semantic Relations*.

G. A. Miller, R. Beckwith, D. Gross C. Fellbaum, and K. Miller. 1990. Introduction to wordnet: an on-line lexical database. *International journal of lexicography*, 3(4):235–244.

J. Ruppenhofer, M. Ellsworth, M. R. L. Petruck, C. R. Johnson, C. F. Baker, and J. Scheffczyk. 2016. *FrameNet II: Extended Theory and Practice*. International Computer Science Institute, Berkeley, California.

I. Stoyanova and S. Leseva. 2020. Beyond lexical and semantic resources: Linking WordNet with FrameNet and enhancing synsets with conceptual frames. *Koeva, S. (ed.) Towards a Semantic Network Enriched with a Variety of Semantic Relations*, pages 21–48.

M. A. Todorova. 2023. Semantic annotation of verbs of contact in bulgarian. *Workshop on Interoperable Semantic Annotation (ISA-19)*, pages 11–17.

M. A. Todorova, T. Dimitrova, and V. Stefanova. 2022. Research on the basic verbal vocabulary in Bulgarian for students in the initial stage of education through online games. *Pedagogika-Pedagogy*, XCIV:896–913.

BanMANI: A Dataset to Identify Manipulated Social Media News in Bangla

Mahammed Kamruzzaman[1], Md. Minul Islam Shovon[2], and Gene Louis Kim[3]

[1,3] University of South Florida , Tampa, FL, USA 33620
[2] Rajshahi University of Engineering & Technology , Rajshahi-6204, Bangladesh
[1,3]{kamruzzaman1, genekim}@usf.edu
[2]mainulislam588@gmail.com

Abstract

Initial work has been done to address fake news detection and misrepresentation of news in the Bengali language. However, no work in Bengali yet addresses the identification of specific claims in social media news that falsely manipulates a related news article. At this point, this problem has been tackled in English and a few other languages, but not in the Bengali language. In this paper, we curate a dataset of social media content labeled with information manipulation relative to reference articles, called BanMANI. The dataset collection method we describe works around the limitations of the available NLP tools in Bangla. We expect these techniques will carry over to building similar datasets in other low-resource languages. BanMANI forms the basis both for evaluating the capabilities of existing NLP systems and for training or fine-tuning new models specifically on this task. In our analysis, we find that this task challenges current LLMs both under zero-shot and fine-tuned settings.[1]

Reference Article

বাংলাদেশের শহরাঞ্চলে স্বাস্থ্যসেবার মান বাড়াতে আরো ১১ কোটি মার্কিন ডলার ঋণসুবিধার অনুমোদন দিয়েছে **এশিয়ান ডেভেলপমেন্ট ব্যাংক (এডিবি)**। বুধবার সংস্থাটির পাঠানো এক সংবাদ বিজ্ঞপ্তিতে এ তথ্য জানানো হয়েছে। ফিলিপাইনভিত্তিক........ (**ET**: The Asian Development Bank (ADB) has approved an additional loan of 110 million US dollars to improve health services in the urban areas of Bangladesh. This information was revealed in a press release sent by the organization on Wednesday. Philippines based......)

Manipulated Social Media Post

বাংলাদেশের শহরাঞ্চলে স্বাস্থ্যসেবার মান বাড়াতে আরো ১১ কোটি মার্কিন ডলার ঋণসুবিধার অনুমোদন দিয়েছে বিশ্বব্যাংক। (**ET**: The World Bank has approved an additional loan of 110 million US dollars to improve health services in urban areas of Bangladesh.)

Non-manipulated Opinion Expressing Social Media Post

বাংলাদেশের জনগণের জন্য সব সময় কাজ করে যাচ্ছে এশিয়ান ডেভেলপমেন্ট ব্যাংক। আমি আশা করি এই ধারা ভবিষ্যতেও চলমান থাকবে। (**ET**: The Asian Development Bank is always working for the people of Bangladesh. I hope that this trend will continue in the future.)

Figure 1: Example of manipulated and non-manipulated social media post with the corresponding reference article. **ET** denotes the English Translation of the given Bangla sentences. In the given example, the Asian Development Bank (highlighted in blue color) is incorrectly referred to as the World Bank (highlighted in red color) in the manipulated post. In the non-manipulated opinion-expressing post, the Asian Development Bank (highlighted in green color) is correctly referred to.

1 Introduction

Misinformation is an increasingly pressing concern in the current social and political landscape where information frequently spreads through social media platforms with few constraints to reflect the information in reliable sources. This is further exacerbated by the presence of "bots" made by malicious actors that are designed to artificially spread ideas that distort reality (Ferrara, 2020; Lei et al., 2023). In order to mitigate this issue, considerable work has been done to identify fake articles (Shu et al., 2020), verifying scientific and encyclopedia claims (Wadden et al., 2020; Thorne et al., 2018), and identifying claims on social media that distort news from trusted sources (Huang et al., 2023). However, most such work is limited to only English.

Bangla, with the fifth-most L1 speakers worldwide, at 233.7 million[2], only has prior work in detecting fake articles (Hossain et al., 2020). More work in this direction is needed

[1]Our dataset is available at https://github.com/kamruzzaman15/BanMANI.

[2]https://en.wikipedia.org/wiki/List_of_languages_by_total_number_of_speakers

Proceedings of the First ConTenNTS Workshop and the 16th BUCC workshop, pages 51–58
Varna, Sep 7, 2023
https://doi.org/10.26615/978-954-452-090-8_007

for Bangla on social media platforms, as demonstrated by the 2012 Ramu incident. In the Ramu incident, a Facebook post from a fake account led to the destruction of a Buddhist temple and dozens of houses in Bangladesh by an angry mob of almost 25,000 people (Ahmed and Manik, 2012). In this vein, we construct a dataset of news-related social media content for identifying news manipulation in social media, `BanMANI`. This dataset is the comparable Bangla counterpart to the ManiTweet dataset (Huang et al., 2023) in English. Figure 1 shows an example of a reference news article alongside both a manipulated and a non-manipulated social media post.

This paper's contributions are the following.

- We construct a publicly available Bangla dataset of 800 news-related social media items that are annotated as manipulated or not relative to 500 reference news articles.
- We present a semi-automatic method for generating such a dataset, which allows scalable dataset collection using annotators efficiently for languages with few available NLP tools.
- We demonstrate that current SOTA LLMs struggle on this task, both in zero-shot and fine-tuned settings.

2 Related Work

This paper is most closely related to fact-checking and fake news detection tasks. While much work in this direction has been done in English, Hossain et al. (2020) only recently started work in this domain in Bangla by releasing a dataset for fake news detection.

In English, Huang et al. (2023) released a dataset for identifying news manipulation in Tweets. In order to supplement fully-human data, they used a semi-automatic approach of generating Tweets using ChatGPT and using human annotators to validate and label the results. They found that ChatGPT and Vicuna failed to solve this new task, even after fine-tuning. In their work, they used `FakeNewsNet` (Shu et al., 2019) dataset to seed their reference articles.

Fact-checking tasks closely resemble our task in that claims must be compared against reference evidence, such as in the FEVER (Thorne et al., 2018) and SCIFACT (Wadden et al., 2020) datasets. Techniques for this kind of fact-checking work often use a retrieval module that pulls relevant data from the supplied candidate pool. The degree of consistency between a piece of evidence and the input claim is then evaluated using a reasoning component (Pradeep et al., 2021).

While our task compares text against a reference article, models must be able to separate social media news related to the reference article from those that only convey opinions to ensure the successful completion of our task. This is the key difference between these (i.e., fact-checking and fake news detection) and our work.

3 Task Definition

Our goal is to identify whether a news-related *social media item* (a post or a comment) is manipulated. If the social media item is manipulated then furthermore to determine what particular information is being manipulated relative to a related reliable reference article. We divide this task into three parts.

Subtask 1. First, we identify whether a particular social media item is manipulated. This part is a binary classification task and we consider an item as manipulated if there is at least one manipulated excerpt.

Subtask 2. Second, if a social media item is classified as manipulated then we need to identify which particular excerpt is manipulated. The task then is to identify the excerpt of the social media item which is not consistent with the original reference news article. In our dataset, we refer to any manipulated or newly introduced span as an *altered excerpt.*

Subtask 3. The third subtask is to identify the part of the original news article which is manipulated in the social media item. In our dataset, we define the information being manipulated as *original excerpt.* Models must produce an empty string or "none" as the output when the *altered excerpt* is inserted without modifying any *original excerpts.*

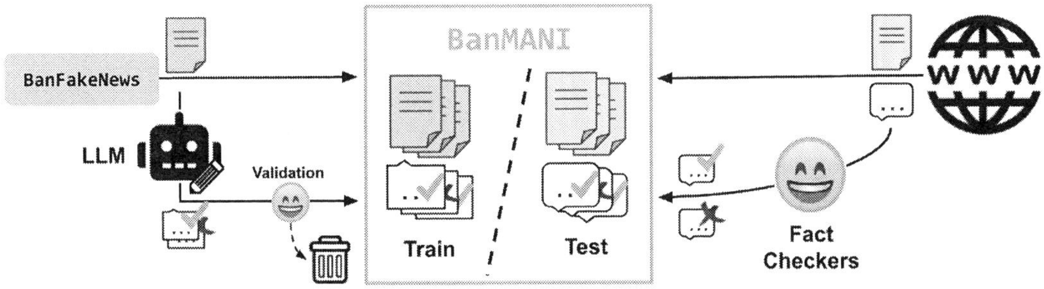

Figure 2: A diagram of the dataset collection procedure. The left side shows the semi-automatic data collection procedure for the training set, seeded by the BanFakeNews dataset (Section 4.3). The right side shows the collection of human-fact-checked items for the test set (Section 4.4).

4 BanMANI: Dataset Creation

We confined our test data collection to Facebook since this platform is more commonly used by Bangla speakers compared to typically studied media platforms for English speakers (e.g., Twitter, Instagram, etc.).[3] We have created a dataset that contains 800 news-related social media items with 500 associated news articles. Our dataset contains 530 manipulated items and 270 non-manipulated items. The breakdown of our dataset is shown in Table 1.

4.1 Bangla-specific Challenges

The task of constructing a Bangla version of the ManiTweet dataset is complicated by several factors. First and foremost, the availability and efficacy of NLP tools in Bangla are much more limited than in English. This means that some reliably automated steps in the English data collection process may be impossible or unreliable in Bangla. In addition to this, a Bangla version of FakeNewsNet (Shu et al., 2020), the dataset that Huang et al. (2023) use as a basis for their ManiTweet dataset, does not exist. FakeNewsNet contains news articles with associated Twitter data which can be directly annotated with any identifiable manipulation. In our dataset construction process, we must identify news articles and corresponding social media posts ourselves since no such seed dataset exists in Bangla.

[3]According to StatCounter.com (https://gs.statcounter.com/), Twitter held 22.01% of thie social media market share in the US in June 2023, but only 1.41% in Bangladesh. On the other hand, Facebook held 48.2% of the market share in the US but 78.84% in Bangladesh.

4.2 Source of News Articles

We collected our news article from BanFakeNews (Hossain et al., 2020), a dataset for Bangla fake news detection. From that dataset, we selected 6 domains where we expect the most social media manipulation to occur: National, International, Politics, Entertainment, Crime, and Finance. From those categories, we selected 2.3k seed news articles, which were used to generate manipulated and non-manipulated social media news. We furthermore upsampled the Politics and Entertainment domains as these were singled out in Huang et al.'s (2023) analysis. For more details on the initial data selection, see Appendix A.

4.3 Social Media Item Generation

No suitable dataset of social media items with corresponding news articles exists in Bangla. In order to efficiently use our limited annotator resources, we deploy a semi-automated data collection process using ChatGPT[4]. We use ChatGPT to generate both manipulated and non-manipulated social media items from a seed news article, which is then validated by human annotators.

4.3.1 Collection of Substitutable Sets

In order to generate manipulated social media items using ChatGPT, we first must identify plausible but incorrect substitutions that can be made in social media items. We collect such possible substitutions through a named entity recognition (NER) tagger. This mirrors the procedure used by Huang et al. (2023). We

[4]GPT-3.5-turbo

Split	Manipulated		Non-manipulated		Total
	Post	Comment	Post	Comment	
Train	370	100	130	50	650
Test	40	20	60	30	150

Table 1: BanMANI Dataset Statistics

collect news-relevant substitutable sets by running a Bangla NER tagger on 2,300 news articles from the BanFakeNews. We consider any two entities with the same NER label as substitutable with each other. We collected all PERSON, ORGANIZATION, and LOCATION named entities from the NER results, following the NER label choices used by Huang et al. (2023).

Based on preliminary experimentation of available Bangla NER systems, we found mBERT-Bengali-NER[5], a BERT-based multilingual Bengali NER system, to perform the best in our use case. Due to the high error rate of Bangla NER taggers, we perform a human filtering step to remove mistakes in the automatic NER labeling. Details of this step are provided in Appendix B.

We supplement the automatically collected entity sets with manually constructed sets of common entity substitutions that were identified in the data construction process. For example, some people write এশিয়ান ডেভেলপমেন্ট ব্যাংক (Asian Development Bank) in their post, when the original news article contains বিশ্বব্যাংক (World Bank). The same interchange also happens for বাংলাদেশ ব্যাংক (Bangladesh Bank) and এশিয়ান ইনফ্রা কচার ইনভেসমেন্ট ব্যাংক (Asian Infrastructure Investment Bank). So we created a substitutable subset inside the ORGANIZATION entity label that contains these four together (এশিয়ান ডেভেলপমেন্ট ব্যাংক, বিশ্বব্যাংক, বাংলাদেশ ব্যাংক, এশিয়ান ইনফ্রা কচার ইনভেসমেন্ট ব্যাংক). Members of these hand-curated sets can similarly be substituted with each other to create manipulated news.

4.3.2 Item Generating Prompts

We use the content attribute of the news articles from the BanFakeNews to create the social media posts and headline attribute of the news articles to create comments. Since comments are generally shorter than posts, we use a different approach to generate them. Social media item generation prompt templates are given in Figure 3.

Non-manipulation prompt for post: You are given a Bangla news article: **BENGALI_NEWS_ARTICLE.** Summarize the article without changing its original meaning and comment about it. Keep it within 250 characters.

Non-manipulation prompt for comment: You are given a Bangla news article: **BENGALI_NEWS_ARTICLE** Summarize the article without changing its original meaning and generate a short headline about it. Keep it within 100 characters.

Manipulation prompt for post: You are given a Bangla news article: **BENGALI_NEWS_ARTICLE.** Summarize and comment on this article but change the **ORIGINAL_EXCERPT** to **ALTERED_EXCERPT** and include **ALTERED_EXCERPT** in your comment. Keep it within 250 characters.

Manipulation prompt for comment: You are given a Bangla news article: **BENGALI_NEWS_ARTICLE.** Summarize and generate a short headline about it but change the **ORIGINAL_EXCERPT** to **ALTERED_EXCERPT** and include **ALTERED_EXCERPT** in your comment. Keep it within 100 characters.

Figure 3: Prompt templates for social media item generation. Here, the "ALTERED EXCERPT" and "ORIGINAL EXCERPT" bear the same meaning as described in Subtask 2 and 3 respectively.

After generating the manipulated and non-manipulated social media items using ChatGPT, we assign human annotators to validate the generated data. The total number of generating manipulated and non-manipulated items using ChatGPT are 2.3k. The generated social media items from ChatGPT are not always coherent or related to the seed news articles. So the human annotators discarded 1.65k generated data during the validation stage. We use the remaining social media items generated by ChatGPT as our training data. In this project, graduate and undergraduate students are working as human annotators. The inter-annotator agreement between the involved annotators is 92.2% per Cohen's kappa (Cohen, 1960). The detailed data annotation process, including screenshots of the annotation inter-

[5] https://huggingface.co/sagorsarker/mbert-bengali-ner

Domain	Manipulated Articles
National	16
International	14
Politics	19
Entertainment	5
Crime	1
Finance	5

Table 2: Manipulated News Articles in Test Data

faces, is available in Appendix C.

4.4 Test Data Collection

We collected 150 human-generated social media items for our test set. These items were collected manually from Facebook using two distinct strategies. In the first strategy, items were sourced from media and news company pages on Facebook, such as Prothom Alo.[6] From these pages, we collected posts that shared a news article with accompanying post text that add commentary as well as comments from the comment sections under news articles on the page. In the second strategy, we collected posts from pages such as BD FactCheck [7] and Rumor Scanner [8] which specialize in identifying fake news published on other platforms.

5 Exploratory Data Analysis

From Table 2, we see most of the manipulated news is political. Some people spread manipulated news on social media to influence public opinion, promote a particular political party, etc., and these might be the reasons behind the manipulated political news. Also, we notice that national and international news are manipulated in a bigger amount. Sites and pages with low trustworthiness are most likely to spread manipulated news. The followers of those sites and pages are most likely unaware of the fact and accidentally post manipulated news.

6 Experimental Setup

6.1 Models

Zero-shot ChatGPT. We use ChatGPT for the zero-shot setting experiments. For details prompt about the zero-shot experiment, see Appendix D.

Fine-tuned. Fine-tuning allows the user to get more out of the available models through provided API. As a result, it can achieve higher quality results than traditional prompt design, train on more examples beyond the limit of traditional prompt, and saves token due to shorter prompts. Fine-tuning improves on few-shot learning by training on much more examples that can fit in a prompt. Which lets you achieve better results in fine-tuned tasks. In general, fine-tuning involves preparing and uploading training data, training the new fine-tuned model with prepared data, and using the fine-tuned model. For our work, we used GPT-3 (Brown et al., 2020) `ada`[9] as our base model due to the unavailability of fine-tuning for the latest models. Also, `ada` is capable of handling simple tasks and is the fastest model in the GPT-3 series. We used a prompt-completion format for our training data and later fine-tuned our model with this data, resulting in competitive outputs.

6.2 Evaluation Metrics

For subtask 1, we use F1 score as this is simply a classification task. Since subtasks 2 and 3 involve span extraction, we use Exact Match (EM) and ROUGE-L (RL).

7 Results & Analysis

The result of the zero-shot ChatGPT and our fine-tuned model is presented in Table 3 and Table 4 respectively. From Table 3 and Table 4, we can see that our fine-tuned model outperforms the zero-shot ChatGPT model for subtask 1, where the F1 score of zero-shot ChatGPT and fine-tuned model is 57.02% and 65.77% respectively. In terms of EM, we can see that our fine-tuned model performs better for both subtask 2 and subtask 3. For subtask 2, if we look at the RL value of our fine-tuned model, we can see that the precision of RL is 69.26%, which is 33.2% more than the zero-shot model. That is also the case for the F1 score of RL. In the same way, for sub-task 3, we can see that the precision and F1 score of RL outperforms the zero-shot model.

[6]https://www.facebook.com/DailyProthomAlo

[7]https://www.facebook.com/bdfactcheck

[8]https://www.facebook.com/RumorScanner

[9]https://platform.openai.com/docs/models

Metric	Subtask 1	Subtask 2	Subtask 3
F1	57.02	--	--
EM	--	8.2	12.3
RL (r, p, f)	--	(79.72, 36.06, 46.83)	(64.78, 41.04, 49.94)

Table 3: Evaluation results of ChatGPT with Zero-shot. Here, EM denotes Exact Match, RL denotes ROUGE-L, which is broken down into (r, p, f) denoting recall, precision, and F1 score respectively.

Metric	Subtask 1	Subtask 2	Subtask 3
F1	65.77	--	--
EM	--	11.9	13.34
RL (r, p, f)	--	(61.95, 69.26, 64.75)	(63.65, 50.74, 56.46)

Table 4: Evaluation result of our fine-tuned GPT-3 model. The table labeling conventions match those of Table 3.

8 Limitations & Future Work

Due to our budget limitation, we were not able to collect a large set of human-written social media items. This means that there exists a gap between the quality of the training and test data; the training set was automatically created, unlike the test data. In the future, we will collect more human-written items from social media to create an entirely human-written training dataset. Our prompts are also purposefully simple, as this was the first step in creating such a dataset. We expect to get qualitative gains in the automatically generated data with more careful prompt engineering. Finally, our experiments were limited to only a single popular LLM for each setting. Expanding the experiments to cover other LLMs, especially open-source LLMs would lead to more robust experimental results and better replicability. We also leave the few-shot method as our future work.

9 Conclusion

In this paper, we presented the BanMANI dataset, the semi-automatically constructed dataset of news manipulation in social media. This dataset extends Huang et al.'s 2023 MANITWEET dataset to Bangla. Our semi-automatic collection process generates social media posts from seed articles using a multilingual LLM and a Bangla NER system. These results are filtered using human annotators for efficient use of annotator time. We find that both zero-shot and fine-tuned LLMs struggle on this dataset, pointing to important directions of future work. Surprisingly, we find that LLMs perform similarly effectively on this dataset when compared to the English variant. We hope that this new resource can help with combating information manipulation in Bangla-speaking social media communities. Furthermore, we believe that the technique laid out here can act as a basis for similar work in other under-served languages in NLP.

References

Inam Ahmed and Julfikar Ali Manik. 2012. A hazy picture appears. [Online; posted 03-October-2012].

Tom B. Brown, Benjamin Mann, Nick Ryder, Melanie Subbiah, Jared Kaplan, Prafulla Dhariwal, Arvind Neelakantan, Pranav Shyam, Girish Sastry, Amanda Askell, Sandhini Agarwal, Ariel Herbert-Voss, Gretchen Krueger, Tom Henighan, Rewon Child, Aditya Ramesh, Daniel M. Ziegler, Jeffrey Wu, Clemens Winter, Christopher Hesse, Mark Chen, Eric Sigler, Mateusz Litwin, Scott Gray, Benjamin Chess, Jack Clark, Christopher Berner, Sam McCandlish, Alec Radford, Ilya Sutskever, and Dario Amodei. 2020. Language models are few-shot learners.

Jacob Cohen. 1960. A coefficient of agreement for nominal scales. *Educational and psychological measurement*, 20(1):37–46.

Emilio Ferrara. 2020. What types of covid-19 conspiracies are populated by twitter bots? *First Monday*, 25(6).

Md Zobaer Hossain, Md Ashraful Rahman, Md Saiful Islam, and Sudipta Kar. 2020. BanFakeNews: A dataset for detecting fake news in Bangla.

In *Proceedings of the Twelfth Language Resources and Evaluation Conference*, pages 2862–2871, Marseille, France. European Language Resources Association.

Kung-Hsiang Huang, Hou Pong Chan, Kathleen McKeown, and Heng Ji. 2023. Manitweet: A new benchmark for identifying manipulation of news on social media.

Zhenyu Lei, Herun Wan, Wenqian Zhang, Shangbin Feng, Zilong Chen, Jundong Li, Qinghua Zheng, and Minnan Luo. 2023. BIC: Twitter bot detection with text-graph interaction and semantic consistency. In *Proceedings of the 61st Annual Meeting of the Association for Computational Linguistics (Volume 1: Long Papers)*, pages 10326–10340, Toronto, Canada. Association for Computational Linguistics.

Ronak Pradeep, Xueguang Ma, Rodrigo Nogueira, and Jimmy Lin. 2021. Scientific claim verification with VerT5erini. In *Proceedings of the 12th International Workshop on Health Text Mining and Information Analysis*, pages 94–103, online. Association for Computational Linguistics.

K. Shu, D. Mahudeswaran, S. Wang, D. Lee, and H. Liu. 2020. FakeNewsNet: A Data Repository with News Content, Social Context, and Spatiotemporal Information for Studying Fake News on Social Media. *Big Data*, 8(3):171–188.

Kai Shu, Deepak Mahudeswaran, Suhang Wang, Dongwon Lee, and Huan Liu. 2019. Fakenewsnet: A data repository with news content, social context and spatialtemporal information for studying fake news on social media.

James Thorne, Andreas Vlachos, Christos Christodoulopoulos, and Arpit Mittal. 2018. FEVER: a large-scale dataset for fact extraction and VERification. In *Proceedings of the 2018 Conference of the North American Chapter of the Association for Computational Linguistics: Human Language Technologies, Volume 1 (Long Papers)*, pages 809–819, New Orleans, Louisiana. Association for Computational Linguistics.

David Wadden, Shanchuan Lin, Kyle Lo, Lucy Lu Wang, Madeleine van Zuylen, Arman Cohan, and Hannaneh Hajishirzi. 2020. Fact or fiction: Verifying scientific claims. In *Proceedings of the 2020 Conference on Empirical Methods in Natural Language Processing (EMNLP)*, pages 7534–7550, Online. Association for Computational Linguistics.

A Initial Data selection Details

Initially (before the first round of human validation) we took 2.3k news articles and generated news-related social media items. In Table 5, we show the details of each category data.

Domain	No. of Articles
National	288
International	288
Politics	690
Entertainment	460
Crime	287
Finance	287

Table 5: Initially Taken News Articles Based on Each Category

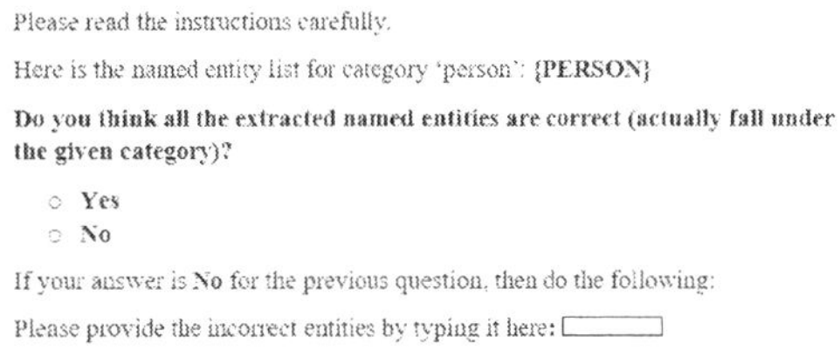
Please read the instructions carefully.

Here is the named entity list for category 'person': {PERSON}

Do you think all the extracted named entities are correct (actually fall under the given category)?

- **Yes**
- **No**

If your answer is No for the previous question, then do the following:

Please provide the incorrect entities by typing it here:

Figure 4: NER Annotation Interface

B NER Annotation Process

Since the performance of the Bangla NER system is not accurate, we need to discard some of the named entities after extracting them. We presented our NER annotation details in Figure 4. In Figure 4, we only show the annotation process for `PERSON` and we do this for every other category (i.e, `ORGANIZATION, and LOCATION`).

C Data Annotation Process

In our research, we perform a two-stage data annotation process for our data. To ensure data quality and consistency, we have selected only those annotators whose mother tongue is Bengali. In this project, all the annotators are graduate and undergraduate students from different institutions. In this project, we have selected a total of 5 students as annotators and kept the data that got at least three annotators' votes.

Stage 1. In the first stage, we asked each annotator to read the generated social media items carefully and see whether it makes sense to them or not and this stage is only limited to our train data. We need to introduce this round because sometimes ChatGPT generates very poor data that doesn't make any sense or totally unrelated to the corresponding news article. Especially the Bangla data generation

Please read the instructions carefully.

Here is the social media post/comment: **{Post/Comment}**

Here is the original reference article: **{Reference News Article}**

Do you think the generated post/comment is closely related to the original reference article?

- ○ **Yes**
- ○ **No**

Figure 5: Stage 1 Annotation.

Please read the instructions carefully.

Here is the social media post/comment: **{Post/Comment}**

Here is the original reference article: **{Reference News Article}**

We made a prediction that this {post/comment} is non-manipulated. Was our prediction accurate?

- ○ **Yes**
- ○ **No**

Figure 6: Stage 2 Annotation for Non-manipulated Social Media Items.

performance of ChatGPT is bad compared to English. So this round of annotation ensures the generated items are not unrelated to the news topic. Figure 5 represents the annotation details of stage 1. We only keep those data that receive a 'Yes' in stage 1.

Stage 2. Here in stage two, we annotated our test and train both data based on manipulated and non-manipulated classes. For the non-manipulation class, we follow the instructions pictured in Figure 6. The annotation interface for the manipulated class is presented in Figure 7. We keep the data that receive a 'Yes' for non-manipulated class. For the manipulated class, we asked a few more questions for annotators because it is difficult to collect manipulated data from social media. If the answer to the first annotation interface question for manipulated class is 'Yes', then we asked two more questions. The purpose of the latter two questions is that if we classified the manipulated post correctly but accidentally got the altered or original excerpt wrong, then the annotators can give us the accurate excerpt and in this way, we can keep the data.

D Zero-shot Prompt for ChatGPT

The zero-shot prompt template for the ChatGPT model is shown in Figure 8.

Please read the instructions carefully.

Here is the social media post/comment: **{Post/Comment}**

Here is the original reference article: **{Reference News Article}**

Predicted original and manipulated fact: **{original --> manipulated}**

We made a prediction that this {post/comment} is manipulated. Was our prediction accurate?

- ○ **Yes**
- ○ **No**

If your answer is **Yes** for the previous question, then answer the following questions:

We made a prediction about the original fact being: {original}. Was our prediction accurate?

- ○ **Yes**
- ○ **No**

If we made an error, please provide the correct original fact by typing it here: [ ]

We made a prediction about the manipulated fact being: {manipulated}. Was our prediction accurate?

- ○ **Yes**
- ○ **No**

If we made an error, please provide the correct manipulated fact by typing it here: [ ]

Figure 7: Stage 2 Annotation for Manipulated Social Media Items.

You need to identify manipulated and non-manipulated social media items. You will be giving a social media item and a reference article.

Your Task:

1. If the social media item is manipulated, then your task is to identify which information from the article is misrepresented by which information in the item. You have to answer in the following format "Manipulating span: **altered_excerpt,** Manipulated span: **original_excerpt**" in a single line. Here, **altered_excerpt** is the new information introduced in the social media item and **original_excerpt** is the original information in the article. If the items imply insert information, {**original_excerpt**} must be "none".

2. If the social media item does not manipulate the article, answer "**no manipulation**". When the item is not manipulated then you don't need to provide the **original_excerpt** and **altered_excerpt**.

No explanation is required for your answer.

Social Media Item: {post or comment}

Reference Article: {article}

Figure 8: Zero-shot Prompt

Supervised Feature-based Classification Approach to Bilingual Lexicon Induction from Specialised Comparable Corpora

Ayla Rigouts Terryn
KU Leuven, Kulak
Centre for Computational Linguistics
ayla.rigoutsterryn@kuleuven.be

Abstract

This study, submitted to the BUCC2023 shared task on bilingual term alignment in comparable specialised corpora, introduces a supervised, feature-based classification approach. The approach employs both static cross-lingual embeddings and contextual multilingual embeddings, combined with surface-level indicators such as Levenshtein distance and term length, as well as linguistic information. Results exhibit improved performance over previous methodologies, illustrating the merit of integrating diverse features. However, the error analysis also reveals remaining challenges.

1 Introduction

The current contribution represents a submission to the BUCC2023 shared task on bilingual term alignment in comparable specialised corpora[1], specifically for the English-French language pair. The task can alternatively be phrased as bilingual lexicon induction (BLI) for terminology. It holds significant potential: it can benefit end-users with ad hoc bilingual terminology construction from relatively easily available comparable corpora, and offers researchers a probing task to assess the cross-lingual lexico-semantic knowledge of language models.

This complex task encompasses many current challenges in natural language processing. First, there are the challenges related to the data. With parallel corpora, identifying an equivalent term in the aligned sentence is, if not simple, at least a task with limited possible answers. With comparable corpora, the task becomes exponentially harder. There is no straightforward place in the corpus to start looking for equivalents, and no guarantee that there will be a valid cross-lingual equivalent for each term. This makes it difficult both to construct a gold standard dataset and to automate the task. For the shared task, the former issue was addressed by creating comparable corpora based on parallel corpora (Adjali et al., 2022b). Moreover, the shared task starts from a predefined list of candidate terms, so the focus is only on the cross-lingual alignment, and not term identification. Besides the data-related challenges, there are conceptual challenges. Terminological equivalence must be defined (Should terms and meanings be considered in context? How close does the meaning have to be, for a term to be considered valid? Do equivalents need to have the same syntactic function or can, e.g., an adjective be a valid equivalent for a noun?). This issue is circumvented in the shared task because the dataset was created based on parallel data, where the equivalence can be defined in context. As will be seen in the error analysis, this also means there are remaining questions as to the equivalence of, for instance, false positives. A final challenge concerns the choice of lexical items, in this case: single- and multi-word terms. Popular embedding-based approaches still struggle with accurate representations for multi-words. Including multi-words alongside single-words, with pairs of different lengths, forces participants to develop a methodology that handles both. For instance, the French equivalent for *train station* is *gare*, and for *database* it is *base de données*. Additionally, terminology is typically not as common as general vocabulary, so methodologies need to be more robust for smaller datasets and lower frequencies.

This paper starts with information on the shared task dataset and setup, and a section on related research. Next, the methodology is described, followed by the results and a brief error analysis, before summarising the findings and looking ahead in the conclusion.

[1] 2023 Building and Using Comparable Corpora shared task website: https://comparable.limsi.fr/bucc2023/bucc2023-task.html

Proceedings of the First ConTenNTS Workshop and the 16th BUCC workshop, pages 59–68
Varna, Sep 7, 2023
https://doi.org/10.26615/978-954-452-090-8_008

2 Dataset and Task

This year's shared task uses an identical setup and dataset to that of last year, so detailed information on the dataset and shared task rules can be found in last year's overview paper (Adjali et al., 2022a). As this was the only submission to this year's shared task, there is no separate overview paper this year, but additional information can be found on the website (see footnote 1). Shared task participants received a comparable corpus in source and target language, as well as lists of terms in source and target language. For the English-French language pair, a gold standard list of equivalents was provided as training data. Thus, the focus of this task is on the cross-lingual alignments. Not all terms in the lists of source and target language terms are present in the cross-lingual gold standard, and some terms have multiple correct equivalents.

Number of:	training	test
tokens in src corp.	19,358,505	4,464,919
tokens in tgt corp.	21,378,916	14,158,415
GS term pairs	2,519	1,970
src terms	3,132	1,270
tgt terms	2,984	9,712
src terms not in txt	17	0
tgt terms not in txt	30	9

Table 1: Number of tokens and terms in source (src) and target language (tgt) parts of the BUCC2023 dataset (tokenisation with spaCy); GS=Gold Standard, txt=text

Looking at the sizes of the datasets (see Table 1), a few things stand out. First, the corpora are quite large, with a slightly larger training corpus than test corpus. Though the source and target language parts of the training corpora are very similar in size, this is not the case for the test data, where the target language part is over three times as large. A second observation is that, for both train and test data, more terms are provided in the target language. However, this difference is once again much larger in the test corpus, with over seven times as many target language terms as source language terms. Third, as indicated, not all terms are included in the gold standard list of pairs. For instance, in the training data, around 80% of all source and target terms occur in the list of gold standard term pairs. One final difference between train and test data stands out: the number of gold standard term pairs in relation to the number of terms in each language. The number of gold standard term pairs is significantly lower than the number of terms in each language in the training data, whereas for the test data, there are more gold standard term pairs than source language terms. All of these differences between training and test data will influence the performance of any supervised system trained on this dataset.

All occurrences of all terms were identified in the lowercased and tokenised corpora. Most, but not all terms were found. In the training data, terms that were not found did not appear in the gold standard list of term pairs. However, in the test data some terms among the gold standard term pairs were not found in the corpus. Therefore, with this methodology, these terms could not be found by the system either. This was only the case for four pairs in the test data. There is a relatively even distribution between single- and multi-word terms in all parts of the corpora: 41% and 61% single-word terms in source and target training data; and 48% and 44% in source and target test data respectively).

The corpora contain texts from many different domains, and they are not very specialised. There are many very general terms (e.g., *water bottle*, *slow*, *remarks*, *young adults*), and much fewer specialised terms (e.g., *sovereignty*, *probiotic*, *legal person*). In both train and test data, there are many instances that would not conventionally be called terms e.g., *whosoever*, *very long time*, *necessarily*, *mere*, *friendly atmosphere*, etc. This is due to the automatic creation of the dataset, based on automatic term extraction with TermSuite (Cram and Daille, 2016). This is not to say that TermSuite's performance is bad, but there will inevitably be errors. Moreover, TermSuite is meant to work well on domain-specific specialised corpora and, while the BUCC corpora are somewhat specialised, they cover many different domains.

A ranked list of term pairs for the test data had to be submitted, with the most confidently predicted pair at the top. Up to five submissions were allowed per team. This list was evaluated through uninterpolated average precision (AP), with an evaluation script provided on GitHub[2].

3 Related Research

Last year, two teams submitted three runs each to this shared task (Adjali et al., 2022a). Team Jozef Stefan Institute (JSI) (Repar et al., 2022) trained an SVM binary classifier (Joachims, 2002), using features based on both the shared task resources,

[2]https://github.com/PierreZweigenbaum/bucc2022

and external (freely available) resources. They originally experimented with cross-lingual embeddings and sentence transformers, but chose a feature-based approach instead, due to unsatisfying results. This approach was based on previous work (Repar et al., 2021), where they incorporated "the cosine similarity values of the crosslingual and sentence transformer models into features of the machine learning model" (Repar et al., 2022, p. 63). They use four types of features. The "cognate-based features" take into account the specific differences between language. For instance, words ending in *-ology* in English are likely to end in *-ologie* in French. Their "dictionary-based features" rely on GIZA++ word alignment (Och and Ney, 2003). The "embedding-based features" use cosine similarity scores from cross-lingually aligned embeddings and five language models. The final group of "combined features" combines parts of all three other groups.

Team CUNI (Požár et al., 2022) submitted three different systems: one with cross-lingually aligned static embeddings, one with contextual multilingual embeddings, and one with unsupervised phrase-based machine translation. For the former, they trained FastText embeddings (Bojanowski et al., 2016) for both languages and aligned them cross-lingually using the MUSE tool (Conneau et al., 2018). For the contextual embeddings they worked with multilingual BERT (Devlin et al., 2019) and XLM (Conneau and Lample, 2019). Finally, they used the Monoses tool (Artetxe et al., 2019) to train an unsupervised phrase-based machine translation model on the provided comparable corpora. They also submitted a combined approach using both the cross-lingually aligned embeddings and phrase-based machine translation.

On the test set, the CUNI team obtained the highest uninterpolated average precision score (0.2816) with their combined system, closely followed by two of the submissions of JSI (0.2685 and 0.2674). Team JSI concluded that "careful feature engineering could still produce better results than more novel deep learning approaches", though they admit their system is "quite resource intensive" (Repar et al., 2022, p. 64). Team CUNI concluded that they were able to get the highest mean average precision (MAP) on the train set with the XLM-model, fine-tuned on the task dataset. The task organisers noticed that 10.7% of the gold standard term pairs were not found by any of the six submitted systems. A recurring issue was when multiple equivalents were present in the gold standard data, and the systems did not find all options. Multi-word terms were also found to be more difficult (Adjali et al., 2022a).

Of course, there is other related research outside of the shared task, though rarely including multi-words. Generally, it is interesting to see experiments where the information from language models is supplemented with additional (linguistic) information. Researchers argue that "there is still room in the NLP toolbox for methods that utilise discrete, symbolic linguistic knowledge; in fact, the two paradigms can be successfully combined for an amplified effect" (Majewska et al., 2022). Specifically for BLI, there is also a call for more rigour on the definition of the task and the used datasets. Laville et al. (2022) address the challenges related to evaluating BLI. Focusing on the popular and valuable MUSE dataset (Conneau et al., 2018), they identify several issues: there is an overrepresentation of proper nouns, of graphically similar (or identical) word pairs, and of high frequency words. A similar argument is made in the work of Kementchedjhieva et al (2019), who, additionally, talk about the gaps in the gold standard datasets. Some of these issues are notably less present in the BUCC shared task dataset because it focuses on terminology, making it more interesting and challenging. Nevertheless, the gold standard data is still automatically generated, so any research requires thorough evaluation that goes beyond simple scores to identify system strengths and weaknesses.

4 Experimental Setup

The methodology of this work is partly inspired by last year's submissions by team JSI (Repar et al., 2022): it is also a feature-based classifier that combines different types of features, including ones based on embeddings. The provided training data was used to train a supervised, binary classifier. Besides the data provided by the shared task, the methodology also relies on pretrained embeddings (no embeddings were trained or fine-tuned on the corpora from the shared task). Additionally, two of the submitted systems were trained on a combination of the provided training data and a supplementary dataset: the Annotated Corpora for Term Extraction Research (ACTER) (Rigouts Terryn et al., 2020), specifically using the cross-lingual annotations in the domain of heart failure as described in Rigouts Terryn et al. (2018). Contrary to the shared task dataset, ACTER contains manual annotations, both for term identification and cross-lingual term alignment. It contains a mix of general and very specific terms, and the corpus is much smaller than that of the shared task (± 60k tokens per language). The English-French part of the dataset contains 2455 term pairs. The monolingual annotations of this dataset are publicly available[3], but the cross-lingual annotations require further validation before being released. Therefore, the methodology does not rely heavily on this dataset, except to test the impact of different training data.

4.1 Preprocessing

The first step in the methodology is the linguistic preprocessing of the corpora, including tokenisation, part-of-speech tagging, lemmatisation, and named entity recognition. This was performed using the English and French NLP pipelines of spaCy (version 3.5.4, *en_core_web_lg* and *fr_core_new_lg*) (Honnibal and Montani, 2017). Once the corpora have been preprocessed, all terms in the term lists are tokenised and mapped to the preprocessed corpora. All data is lowercased, but otherwise only exact matches are included. As discussed, not all terms were found in the corpus (see Table 1), and those that were not were excluded from this step onwards. Next, features were calculated for each possible term pair. With 3,115 English and 2,954 French terms remaining in the dataset, this meant 9,201,701 possible term pairs, with only 2519 (0.027%) positive (equivalent) instances. While some basic filters were applied afterwards to reduce this size, calculating all features and training remain computationally intense.

4.2 Features

cross-lingually aligned static embeddings (1) The strategy for the alignment of the static embeddings was based on previous research (Singh et al., 2022) on the improvement of domain-specific cross-lingual embeddings. For the monolingual embeddings, the same setup is used as in the previous study: FastText (Bojanowski et al., 2016), pretrained on the Common Crawl corpus and Wikipedia. "These models were trained using the Continuous Bag of Words (CBOW) model with position weights, a dimensionality of 300, character n-grams of length 5, a window of size 5, and 10 negative samples" (Singh et al., 2022, p. 128). The monolingual embeddings were aligned using VecMap (Artetxe et al., 2018). As shown in the study by Singh et al., cross-lingually aligned embeddings rely heavily on a relevant seed lexicon for the alignment. In their study, the lexicon was automatically constructed based on Wikipedia titles and the cross-lingual Wikipedia links. For the shared task, this approach could not easily be used, because the data is not limited to a single domain. Nevertheless, it was felt that including more specialised vocabulary in the seed dictionary could be beneficial. For the seed lexicon in the current study, the MUSE dataset (Conneau et al., 2018) was taken as a starting point. Though the quality of the English-French MUSE dataset was found to be high for the most frequent words, it was still manually amended (no automatic filtering was performed). This mainly meant removing some named entities to balance out their overrepresentation, focusing on those named entities that would be much more commonly used in English than in French, such as the names of the US states. A few errors were also removed. Starting from the MUSE list of 113,286 word pairs, 10,021 of the most common pairs were maintained. Additionally, 600 medical single-word medical term pairs from the work of Singh et al. (2022) were included. Finally, almost 1500 more single-word terms were manually added from diverse domains, based on the following online resources: Dictionnaire de l'Académie Nationale de Médicine[4] (379 term pairs), Anglais Pratique[5] (819 term pairs, including chemical elements and biological terms), and Lexique anglais-français d'écologie numérique et de statistique[6] (Legendre and Legendre, 1999) (285 terms from statistics). This resulted in a seed lexicon of 12,104 word pairs in total.

In the training dataset, there were no out-of-vocabulary terms; in the test dataset there were seven in English and thirteen in French (a possible indication that the test data is slightly more specialised than the training data). For multi-word terms, the token embeddings were combined using mean pooling, and only if at least half of the tokens were in-vocabulary. This was to avoid cases where embeddings only existed for the common

[3]https://github.com/AylaRT/ACTER

[4]http://dictionnaire.academie-medecine.fr/

[5]https://anglais-pratique.fr/

[6]http://www.numericalecology.com/lex/index.html

parts of the multi-word term, and not for the more meaningful part(s). This could be especially important in French, where multi-word terms are regularly connected by prepositions or articles (e.g., *environmental protection* in French is *protection de l'environnement*). FastText cosine similarity score was included as a single feature. In the case of out-of-vocabulary terms, average BERT cosine similarity (see next section) was taken instead.

multilingual contextual embeddings (5 or 3) The contextual embeddings of choice were pretrained multilingual BERT embeddings (Devlin et al., 2019), accessed through Hugging Face Transformers (Wolf et al., 2020-07-13). Again, the mean of the token embeddings is used for terms that contain multiple tokens. Five contexts were selected per term, evenly divided over the corpus. This strategy was meant to increase the possibility of finding the term in different informative contexts, without increasing the computational load too much by getting embeddings for all occurrences of all terms. For each term pair, five cosine similarity scores were calculated between the five embeddings for source and target terms. The official submissions to the shared task use these five features. However, it was then observed that including five cosine similarity scores from randomly selected contexts might not be ideal, as there is no telling which of the five will be more informative. Therefore, for subsequent experiments, the five original features were turned into three more interpreted ones: minimum, mean, and maximum cosine similarity scores (out of the original five).

edit distance (1) For the English-French dataset, edit distance could clearly be a relevant feature for many (though certainly not all) term pairs. Only Levenshtein distance (Levenshtein, 1966) was included as a feature, but more advanced implementations, e.g., like the cognate-based features of Repar et al. (2022), might be considered in the future.

frequency (6) Relative frequencies of the source and target terms in the term pair were included as well, with both the relative frequencies of the full forms and the lemmas. Additionally, the difference between the relative frequencies for full forms and lemmas was included as well, resulting in six frequency-related features. These will be more relevant for more comparable corpora, and less so for corpora that are more different in each language.

length (8) The length of source and target terms, measured in tokens and in characters, was included as well, alongside features with the difference (length source term minus length target term) and ratio (length source term divided by sum of length source term and length target term) between these lengths. This results in eight length-related features: four counting tokens, four with characters.

linguistic information (26) The most commonly assigned (out of five contexts) part-of-speech pattern (single tag in case of single-word terms) and named entity recognition label was obtained for each term. These were turned into numeric features in several ways. For the part-of-speech patterns, the five potentially most informative tags were selected: adjective, adverb, noun, proper noun, and verb. For all of these, the numbers of tokens with that tag in source and target terms were added as features, as well as the difference and ratio between the counts for source and target terms. This means that, for each of the five selected tags, four features were calculated (number of tokens with tag in source term, number of tokes with tag in target term, difference between these two, and ratio between these two), adding up to twenty part-of-speech features. Three additional part-of-speech features were added: (1) whether or not the pattern is identical for source and target terms, (2) whether or not the tags (regardless of their order) are identical for source and target terms, and (3) how many tags only occur in either source or target term. Finally, three more named entity recognition features are added: the average number of tokens of the source and target terms tagged as a named entity (across five contexts), and the difference between these averages for source and target terms. In total, there are 26 linguistic features.

4.3 Filtering

The resulting term pairs with features were filtered, e.g., removing any pairs with a FastText cosine similarity below 0.1, an average BERT cosine similarity below 0.1, or a very large difference in length (e.g., over 30 characters). The filters were intentionally set very broadly, so that no positive equivalents were removed from the training data. This means a very large number remains for training and classification (8,391,279). These filters could be set more strictly without losing (much) accuracy in the training data. Even so, 19 equivalent term pairs were removed from the test data with the broad

submission	Training data	Scoring	# predictions	AP	P	R	F1
1	BUCC-train + ACTER	f1_weighted	790	.30	.82	.33	.47
2	BUCC-train + ACTER	roc	1606	**.42**	.60	.49	.54
3	BUCC-train	f1_weighted	785	.30	.82	.32	.46
4	BUCC-train	roc	1205	.39	.71	.43	.54

Table 2: Details of the submitted systems, including the training data and scoring metric used for optimisation, as well as official results in terms of uninterpolated average precision (AP), precision (P), recall (R), and F1-score (F1)

filter, further illustrating the differences between the datasets.

4.4 Classifier

The experiments were performed in Scikit-learn (Pedregosa et al., 2011) with the Random Forest Classifier (Ho, 1995). This choice was motivated by its relative efficiency, interpretability, and the options to get probability scores for each prediction and estimate the importance of each feature. All features were scaled using the *StandardScaler*. Limited hyperparameter optimisation was used for the systems submitted to the shared task for the hyperparameters *min_sample_leaf*, *min_sample_split*, and *n_estimators*. For the remaining experiments in this contribution, no more optimisation was used and hyperparameters were set to: *class_weight='balanced', min_samples_leaf=5, min_samples_split=5, n_estimators=500*. Optimisation was either based on weighted f1-score (f1_w), or on Area Under the Receiver Operating Characteristic Curve (roc).

4.5 Data for Experiments

Four systems were officially submitted with the settings detailed in Table 2, and 47 features. These systems were trained on either the provided training data, or a combination of that training data with the ACTER dataset. Predictions were sorted based on the predicted probability of equivalence. Only positively predicted pairs were included (predicted probability of equivalence at least 50%), but this threshold could easily be adapted to favour either precision or recall.

Further experiments were performed after the official submissions. These used the three adapted features for cosine similarity from contextual embeddings (min, mean, and max cosine distance based on five contexts) and no hyperparameter optimisation. A first batch of experiments used just the BUCC training dataset, which was split into a separate train and test set. This was done by splitting the gold standard into 80% training pairs and 20% test pairs, and then splitting off the term pairs with features based on whether the source term was in the test set. The final batch of experiments used the same settings on the test data, which was made available by the organisers.

5 Results

The official results for the shared task can be found in Table 2. Though there were no other participants for a comparison this year, there is a considerable improvement over last year's top score of 0.28 AP. The best results were obtained by a system trained on a combination of the BUCC and the ACTER datasets, and optimised for roc. The addition of the ACTER dataset did not appear to have a big influence on the scores, but optimising for roc clearly worked better than optimising for f1_weighted. Precision scores are much higher than recall in all submitted systems, and many equivalent pairs could still be found below the threshold of 50% predicted confidence of equivalence, meaning that scores might be further improved by lowering the threshold.

As described, further experiments were performed to analyse the system and results in more detail. The experiments focused on the impact of: the scoring used for optimisation, the features, and the threshold value (i.e., the minimum predicted probability score for equivalence). Originally, this threshold was always set at 50% (only pairs the system actually predicted as equivalent), but since it was observed that uninterpolated average precision could be further improved by lowering this threshold, scores were also calculated at a cut-off point of 25%. For each experiment, uninterpolated average precision (AP) is reported as defined by shared task, as well as precision (P), recall (R), and F1-score (F1). Additionally, F1-score of the true label in the classification task (F1_true) is included, and the number of predicted equivalent pairs above the threshold (#),

Concerning the **features**, experiments were per-

train data	score	features	F1_ true	threshold@50%					threshold@25%				
				#	AP	P	R	F1	#	AP	P	R	F1
experiments on train data (80/20-split)													
BUCC	f1_w	all	.80	618	.82	.72	.88	.79	946	.86	.50	.94	.65
BUCC	roc	all	.81	612	.82	.72	.88	.79	950	**.87**	.50	.94	.65
BUCC	f1_w	cos	.71	647	.70	.62	.80	.70	958	.74	.45	.86	.59
BUCC	roc	cos	.70	655	.70	.61	.80	.69	956	.73	.45	.85	.59
BUCC	f1_w	cos&lev	.77	622	.77	.69	.85	.76	867	.80	.52	.89	.66
BUCC	roc	cos&lev	.77	624	.78	.69	.85	.76	875	.81	.52	.90	.66
BUCC	f1_w	limited	.83	599	.83	.75	.89	**.82**	864	.86	.54	.93	.69
BUCC	roc	limited	.83	598	**.84**	.75	.89	**.82**	846	.86	.55	.93	.69
experiments on test data													
BUCC+ ACTER	roc	all	.52	1177	.36	.69	.41	.52	2610	**.46**	.45	.60	.51
BUCC	roc	all	.52	1127	.36	.71	.41	.52	2355	**.46**	.47	.56	.51
BUCC	roc	limited	.52	1142	**.37**	.71	.41	.52	2065	.45	.52	.54	**.53**
BUCC	roc	cos	.39	1009	.24	.58	.30	.39	2132	.29	.37	.40	.39

Table 3: Results of further experiments on training data (80/20-split) and on test data

formed with: all described features (**all**: 45 features), only the cosine similarity features and Levenshtein distance (**cos&lev**; 5 features), only the cosine similarity features (**cos**: 4 features), or a limited set of features, including cos & lev, the difference in frequency, the four combined length features, the three part-of-speech features that are not about specific tags, and the difference in the average number of tokens recognised as named entities (**limited**: 14 features). The latter was meant to reduce some of the redundant information in the features, as there were many with both separate values for source and target terms, as well as a feature combining that information.

The results of these additional experiments can be seen in Table 3. The minor difference in setup for experiments with the test data as compared to the submitted runs (different features for contextual embeddings and no hyperparameter optimisation) results in slightly different, but still similar, scores for otherwise comparable experiments.

The first observation about the results in Table 3 is that all scores are much higher for experiments on a train/test-split of the training data, than for experiments trained on the training data and evaluated on the test data. While some deviation is to be expected, as discussed, there are significant differences between training and test datasets. Where AP scores were up to 0.87 for the training experiments, the highest score obtained on the test data is significantly lower at 0.46. A similar drop is seen for the F1-scores. For the experiments with threshold 50%, recall is only half of what it was for the training experiments. And though it is increased with a lower threshold, it is nowhere near the very high recall of 0.94 for the first experiments. Similar differences with results were reported last year. Despite the lower scores compared to the experiments on the training data, the top score of 0.46 AP is much higher than the best score of .28 submitted to the shared task last year.

The next observation is that a lower threshold results in (much) higher scores for AP. For the experiments on the training data, this improvement in AP is due to an increase in recall (up to .94), but the drop in precision results in a lower F1-score. For the experiments on the test data, AP is also highest with the lower threshold thanks to an improved recall, but in this case, the F1-scores are not much affected. Lowering the threshold has a higher impact on the number of predictions for the test data experiments. For the training data experiments, only 245 to 338 more pairs are extracted (+39% to 55%), whereas for the experiments on the test data, lowering the threshold results in up to 1433 more pairs, i.e., an increase of up to 122%. Being able to easily adjust this threshold depending on the requirements of the experiment is a considerable advantage.

Conversely to the results of the officially submitted runs, scoring used for optimisation has only a very minor impact, so, for the experiments on the

feature	importance
cos. sim. FastText	0.373
max. cos. sim. BERT	0.229
mean cos. sim. BERT	0.152
min. cos. sim. BERT	0.104
same POS tags	0.042
Levenshtein distance	0.034
difference in POS	0.015
length tokens ratio	0.013
same POS pattern	0.011
length chars ratio	0.007
length tokens difference	0.006
length chars difference	0.005
frequency difference	0.005
named entity rec. difference	0.002

Table 4: Importance of features limited features

test data, all training was optimised with roc. Predictably, the features do influence results. Clearly and unsurprisingly, the cosine features are most important, and results are not bad with just those features. The addition of Levenshtein is, predictably, an advantage for the English-French language pair as well. Interestingly, the other features also add relevant information, though the individual features are much less important. The system with more limited features appears to efficiently capture the relevant information.

Feature importance scores of a system trained with limited features and optimised with roc are shown in table 4. FastText cosine similarity score is the most important feature by some margin, followed by the three BERT cosine features which, together, are even more important. None of the other features are very important by themselves. Interestingly, the feature indicating whether source and target terms have the same part-of-speech tags (regardless of order) is more important than Levenshtein distance. In conclusion, these experiments show very promising results, especially for systems where training and test data are very similar.

6 Error Analysis

The output of the system trained on the shared task training data and tested on the test data (including all features) was analysed in more detail. Among the most confidently predicted pairs, there is a good mix of single- and multi-word terms, so not all multi-word term pairs were difficult to predict correctly. At the top of this list, there are a lot of pairs with a low Levenshtein distance, though not exclusively. For instance, at rank 7 there is the pair *typical recipe* and *recette typique*, and at rank 31 *disabled children* and *enfants handicapés*. The first false positive is found at rank 74, where *economic difficulties* is aligned with *problèmes économiques* (literally *economic problems*). While a more literal equivalent is available, this pair could certainly be considered equivalent in many contexts. This is seen for many of the highly ranked false positives: they either could be equivalent in certain contexts, or they should have been considered equivalents in the first place, e.g., *strategic game* and *jeu stratégique*, and *direct taxes* and *taxes directes*. Out of 1127 ranked equivalents, there were 325 false positives and 58 of those could be considered equivalent in many contexts, with an additional 33 deemed strongly related or potentially equivalent in some contexts. While these results require a more thorough analysis (with inter-annotator agreement), these numbers are an indication of the importance of a nuanced definition of equivalence and a thorough error analysis.

Naturally, some terms are also clearly misaligned. One of the, probably less serious, common misalignments is between terms with a different number. For instance, the singular *tumor* is aligned with the plural *tumeurs*, and the reverse is done for *wine bottles* and *bouteille de vin*. There are also a few false positives due to different parts-of-speech, for instance, *infected* was matched to *infection*. However, this only occurred eight times, so the part-of-speech features may have already prevented some of these mismatches. Multi-word terms with relatively general words were also found to be difficult. The term *access control system* was linked to 16 different French terms with a probability of at least 25%. A couple of other categories of terms that cause multiple false positives are: numbers, family relations, and colours. For instance, *eighth* is most confidently correctly aligned with *huitième*, but then also (with much lower probability) to *dix-septième* (*seventeenth*). Similarly, *aunt* is correctly matched to *tante* with a 94% probability, but then also to *oncle* (*uncle*) (91%), *mère* (*mother*) (86%), *père* (*father*) (71%), *neveu* (*nephew*) (69%), and so on. Similar issues are found for colours. Sometimes cultural differences play a role, for instance when *pound* is wrongly, but understandably, matched to *kilo*. While performance on multi-word terms was not especially bad, the rather simplistic approach of averaging embeddings has clear downsides. This can be seen in misalignments where word order plays a role, e.g., *wine bottles* is misaligned to *vin en bouteille* (*botteled wine*), and *product safety* to *produits de sécurité* (*safety products*).

7 Conclusion

This contribution to the BUCC2023 shared task on bilingual term alignment in comparable specialised corpora presents a supervised approach with a feature-based classifier that combines features from embeddings with other information, including edit distance and linguistic characteristics. Results are promising and the system outperforms those from last year's submissions. Though the efficient random forest classifier is used, preparing the experiments is, admittedly, computationally expensive, since all source language terms are matched with all target language terms, and contextual features are calculated for each pair. However, it also provides interesting insights, for instance showing the relative importance of the various features. The error analysis illustrates various challenges, both in terms of the dataset and in terms of system weaknesses. Future research is planned to look into rich datasets for BLI from specialised corpora, to facilitate more thorough work on this task. Further experiments will include more features and compare different embeddings, as well as experiments with different types of classifiers. A more elaborate error analysis and the inclusion of more language pairs could further improve our understanding of the cross-lingual knowledge captured (or not) by both static and contextual embeddings.

References

Omar Adjali, Emmanuel Morin, Serge Sharoff, Reinhard Rapp, and Pierre Zweigenbaum. 2022a. Overview of the 2022 BUCC Shared Task- Bilingual Term Alignment in Comparable Specialized Corpora. In *Proceedings of the 15th Workshop on Building and Using Comparable Corpora (BUCC 2022) @LREC2022*, pages 67–76, Marseille, France. European Language Resources Association.

Omar Adjali, Emmanuel Morin, and Pierre Zweigenbaum. 2022b. Building Comparable Corpora for Assessing Multi-Word Term Alignment. In *Proceedings of the 13th Conference on Language Resources and Evaluation (LREC 2022)*, pages 3103–3112, Marseille, France. European Language Resources Association.

Mikel Artetxe, Gorka Labaka, and Eneko Agirre. 2018. A Robust Self-Learning Method for Fully Unsupervised Cross-Lingual Mappings of Word Embeddings. In *Proceedings of the 56th Annual Meeting of the Association for Computational Linguistics (Volume 1: Long Papers)*, pages 789–798, Melbourne, Australia. Association for Computational Linguistics.

Mikel Artetxe, Gorka Labaka, and Eneko Agirre. 2019. An Effective Approach to Unsupervised Machine Translation. In *Proceedings of the 57th Annual Meeting of the Association for Computational Linguistics*, pages 194–203, Florence, Italy. Association for Computational Linguistics.

Piotr Bojanowski, Edouard Grave, Armand Joulin, and Tomas Mikolov. 2016. Enriching Word Vectors with Subword Information.

Alexis Conneau and Guillaume Lample. 2019. Cross-lingual Language Model Pretraining. In *Proceedings of the 33rd Conference on Neural Information Processing Systems (NeurIPS 2019)*, pages 7059–7069, Vancouver, Canada.

Alexis Conneau, Guillaume Lample, Marc'Aurelio Ranzato, Ludovic Denoyer, and Hervé Jégou. 2018. Word Translation Without Parallel Data.

Damien Cram and Beatrice Daille. 2016. TermSuite: Terminology Extraction with Term Variant Detection. In *Proceedings of the 54th Annual Meeting of the Association for Computational Linguistics: System Demonstrations*, pages 13–18, Berlin, Germany. Association for Computational Linguistics.

Jacob Devlin, Ming-Wei Chang, Kenton Lee, and Kristina Toutanova. 2019. BERT: Pre-training of Deep Bidirectional Transformers for Language Understanding.

Tin Kam Ho. 1995. Random decision forests. In *Proceedings of 3rd International Conference on Document Analysis and Recognition*, volume 1, pages 278–282. IEEE.

Matthew Honnibal and Ines Montani. 2017. spaCy 2: Natural language understanding with Bloom embeddings, convolutional neural networks and incremental parsing.

Thorsten Joachims. 2002. *Learning to Classify Text Using Support Vector Machines*. Springer US, Boston, MA.

Yova Kementchedjhieva, Mareike Hartmann, and Anders Søgaard. 2019. Lost in Evaluation: Misleading Benchmarks for Bilingual Dictionary Induction. In *Proceedings of the 2019 Conference on Empirical Methods in Natural Language Processing and the 9th International Joint Conference on Natural Language Processing (EMNLP-IJCNLP)*, pages 3334–3339, Hong Kong, China. Association for Computational Linguistics.

Martin Laville, Emmanuel Morin, and Philippe Langlais. 2022. About Evaluating Bilingual Lexicon Induction. In *Proceedings of the 15th Workshop on Building and Using Comparable Corpora (BUCC 2022) @LREC2022*, pages 8–14, Marseille, France. European Language Resources Association.

Pierre Legendre and Louis Legendre. 1999. Lexique anglais-français d'écologie numérique et de statistique — English-French vocabulary of numerical ecology and statistics.

V.I. Levenshtein. 1966. Binary Codes Capable of Correcting Deletions, Insertions and Reversals. 10(8):707–710.

Olga Majewska, Ivan Vulić, and Anna Korhonen. 2022. *Linguistically Guided Multilingual NLP: Current Approaches, Challenges, and Future Perspectives*, 1 edition, pages 163–188. CRC Press.

Franz Josef Och and Hermann Ney. 2003. A Systematic Comparison of Various Statistical Alignment Models. 29(1):19–51.

Fabian Pedregosa, Gael Varoquaux, Alexandre Gramfort, Vincent Michel, Bertrand Thirion, Olivier Grisel, Mathieu Blondel, Peter Prettenhofer, Ron Weiss, Vincent Dubourg, Jake Vanderplas, Alexandre Passos, and David Cournapeau. 2011. Scikit-learn: Machine Learning in Python. (12):2825–2830.

Borek Požár, Klara Tauchmanová, Kristyna Neumannová, Ivana Kvapilíková, and Ondřej Bojar. 2022. CUNI Submission to the BUCC 2022 Shared Task on Bilingual Term Alignment. In *Proceedings of the 15th Workshop on Building and Using Comparable Corpora (BUCC 2022) @LREC2022*, pages 43–49, Marseille, France. European Language Resources Association.

Andraz Repar, Senja Pollak, Matej Ulčar, and Boshko Koloski. 2022. Fusion of Linguistic, Neural and Sentence-Transformer Features for Improved Term Alignment. In *Proceedings of the 15th Workshop on Building and Using Comparable Corpora (BUCC 2022) @LREC2022*, pages 61–66, Marseille, France. European Language Resources Association.

Andraž Repar, Matej Martinc, Matej Ulčar, and Senja Pollak. 2021. Word-embedding Based Bilingual Terminology Alignment. In *Proceedings Electronic Lexicography in the 21st Century (eLex 2021) Post-editing Lexicography*, page 98.

Ayla Rigouts Terryn, Véronique Hoste, and Els Lefever. 2018. A Gold Standard for Multilingual Automatic Term Extraction from Comparable Corpora: Term Structure and Translation Equivalents. In *Proceedings of the Eleventh International Conference on Language Resources and Evaluation (LREC)*, pages 1803–1808, Miyazaki, Japan. European Language Resources Association.

Ayla Rigouts Terryn, Véronique Hoste, and Els Lefever. 2020. In No Uncertain Terms: A Dataset for Monolingual and Multilingual Automatic Term Extraction from Comparable Corpora. 54(2):385–418.

Pranaydeep Singh, Ayla Rigouts Terryn, and Els Lefever. 2022. Improving Domain-specific Cross-lingual Embeddings with Automatically Generated Bilingual Dictionaries. 12:124–140.

Thomas Wolf, Lysandre Debut, Victor Sanh, Julien Chaumond, Clement Delangue, Anthony Moi, Pierric Cistac, Tim Rault, Rémi Louf, Morgan Funtowicz, Joe Davison, Sam Shleifer, Patrick von Platen, Clara Ma, Yacine Jernite, Julien Plu, Canwen Xu, Teven Le Scao, Sylvain Gugger, Mariama Drame, Quentin Lhoest, and Alexander M. Rush. 2020-07-13. HuggingFace's Transformers: State-of-the-art Natural Language Processing.

Author Index

Association for Computational Linguistics
209 N. Eighth Street
Stroudsburg, Pennsylvania 18360

ISBN 978-1-7138-9042-3

CURRAN ASSOCIATES INC.
proceedings.com